# A TRAVELER'S GUIDE TO
# PIONEER JEWISH CEMETERIES
## OF THE
# CALIFORNIA GOLD RUSH

*By Susan Morris*

COMMISSION FOR THE PRESERVATION OF PIONEER
JEWISH CEMETERIES AND LANDMARKS
Judah L. Magnes Museum
Berkeley, California
1996

*Publication of this book was made possible by a grant from the L.J. Skaggs and Mary C. Skaggs Foundation.*

Book design: Sara Glaser

Street and area maps: Reproduced with permission of copyright owner, Compass Maps, Inc., Modesto, CA 95351.

Illustrations: "Drawn and copied by Miss Lesley Jones, Sacramento, California." From the *Autobiography of Charles Peters, 1915.* The La Grave Publishers, San Francisco.

Published by the Judah L. Magnes Museum 2911 Russell Street, Berkeley, CA 94705

ISBN 0-943376-63-7
Library of Congress Catalog Card No: 95-080185

# ❧ ACKNOWLEDGMENTS ❧

There are many people whom I wish to thank for their contributions to this guide. Without the generous assistance of all those listed below, the guide would still be a work in progress. I am most grateful for the support, encouragement, and expertise of all who helped make the dream a reality.

First and foremost, it is because of the vision and efforts of the Commission for the Preservation of Pioneer Jewish Cemeteries and Landmarks that the pioneer Jewish cemeteries of Sonora, Mokelumne Hill, Jackson, Placerville, Nevada City, and Grass Valley, and Marysville have been restored and preserved as historic and sacred sites. In particular, special recognition is given to the founding trustees for their vision, to Judah L. Magnes Museum Director and Commission Secretary Seymour Fromer, and to Commission Chairperson Stephen A. Zellerbach for his many years of dedication and leadership.

Dr. Robert E. Levinson's work, *The Jews in the California Gold Rush,* served as a major resource for this guide. For at least twenty years prior to his untimely death in 1980, Dr. Levinson meticulously researched and documented the communities and the lives of Jewish Gold Rush pioneers, includ-ing a 1963 study of four Gold Country cemeteries. Dr. Levinson served as executive vice-chairperson of the Commission for more than a decade.

Compass Maps has generously contributed the use of its maps for the guide, and in addition will identify the pioneer Jewish cemeteries on their maps of the Gold Country.

The Western Jewish History Center of the Judah L. Magnes Museum was a key resource for the documents needed to produce this guide. I am most grateful to my colleagues for their continued support and in particular to Ruth Rafael, head archivist emerita, for many things, not the least of which are her extensive knowledge of available sources and her willing-ness to read and edit the manu-script. I am appreciative of the support of Professor Moses Rischin, Director of the Western

Sonora Hebrew Cemetery, circa 1970. Stephen Zellerbach, Chair Cemetery Commis-sion, on left, with Julius Baer at the Baer grave-stone. Commission for the Preservation of Pioneer Jewish Cemeteries and Landmarks Collection, Western Jewish History Center.

Rabbi Joseph B. Glaser, founding member of the Commission for the Preservation of Pioneer Jewish Cemeteries and Landmarks, saying *kaddish* at a pioneer grave site. Courtesy of Sara Glaser.

Jewish History Center. My heartfelt thanks go to Tova Gazit, head archivist, who provided ongoing encouragement, all of the Hebrew translations, and assistance with the section on the *Kaddish*; to Laura O'Hara, photo archivist, for her invaluable assistance in locating appropriate photographs for the guide and for her continued professional approach in the matter of photo archives; and to Ava F. Kahn, research associate, for her professional advice and most of all for her months of suggesting resources and sharing her findings as she worked on her forthcoming publication, *California Jewry: The Gold Rush Years, A Documentary Reader*. In particular, her discussion of Hannah Gumpert, buried in Sonora Hebrew Cemetery, underscored the need for more research regarding women's experiences in the California Gold Rush, and brought to the fore the scarcity of original source material documenting women's lives.

I am most grateful to Paula Naomi Friedman, copy editor for this guide, who, in addition to her work as Judah L. Magnes Museum director of public relations, was invaluable to me because of her writing and editing skills, her sensitivity to the material and the audience, and her sense of humor. I am also very appreciative of the fine work of Laura O'Hara, who performed the final stage of proofreading the manuscript. Nelda Cassuto and Ruth Steiner each made many excellent contributions to the manuscript with skilled proofreading and editing. In addition, the following generous individuals contributed their time and skills in proofreading and content editing: Rose Levine, Ava Kahn, Kathy Morris, Mark Morris, Richard and Ruth Rafael, and Jean Solomon.

Many thanks are due members of the staff of the Judah L. Magnes

Museum for their assistance in making the guide a reality—in particular, Lisbeth Schwab, Marni Welch, and Valerie Huaco.

The following people and institutions provided invaluable assistance and resource material on the lives of those interred in the cemeteries and on local community history: Dick Marquette, Marysville historian; Michel Janicot, Nevada City and Grass Valley historian; Commission members Abraham Friedman; Paul and Jean Solomon; and the staffs of the Amador County Museum, the Tuolumne County Museum, and the Columbia State Historical Park Archives.

Throughout the years many individuals and organizations, including synagogues, youth groups, and community centers, have volunteered their services to preserve and maintain the cemeteries. Now, there is a new generation of Jews living in the Gold Country and the following active and growing organizations assist the Commission in caring for these sacred grounds: Congregation B'nai Harim, Placerville, Foothill Jewish Community of Amador County, Mother Lode Havurah of Tuolumne County, and the Nevada County Jewish Community.

Special recognition is given to Sara Glaser, the designer of this guide. Sara grew up visiting and caring for these pioneer cemeteries, as her father, the late and beloved Rabbi Joseph Glaser, was a founding trustee of the Commission and served for many years as its chairperson and, later, executive vice-chairperson.

I am grateful to Betsy Klein Schwartz for her meticulous research into the Cincinnati-Placerville connections with regard to our mutual pioneer families, Kahn and Hilp, and her Tannenwald and Raphael families.

To my family—Mark, Kathy, and Steve Morris, Barbara Smith, Karen Kistner, your patience, advice (sometimes heeded, sometimes not), sense of humor and perspective are always needed and valued. Thank you.

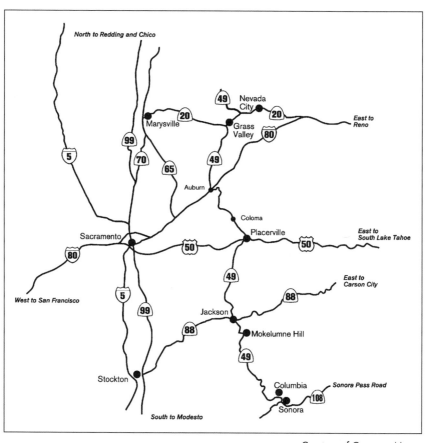

North to Redding and Chico

Marysville

Nevada City

Grass Valley

East to Reno

Auburn

Coloma

Placerville

East to South Lake Tahoe

Sacramento

West to San Francisco

East to Carson City

Jackson

Mokelumne Hill

Stockton

Columbia

Sonora

Sonora Pass Road

South to Modesto

Courtesy of Compass Maps.

# ❧ CONTENTS ❧

Above: Givoth Olam Cemetery, Jackson. Photo: Ira Nowinksi/Judah L. Magnes Museum.
Western Jewish History Center. Right: George Morris. Chinese Camp, circa 1890. Photo Archive
Collection, Western Jewish History Center.

---

### ❧ AUTHOR'S NOTE ❧

---

Often, when I tell people about my work on a guide to California's pioneer Jewish cemeteries, they look at me and ask "Are there any important, famous people buried there?" They seem to expect a glittering list, one that would give them a point of reference and immediate reason for visiting these graves. I understand the question but cannot respond in kind, for I don't think of these historic cemeteries in terms of the *important*.

*All* interred in these sacred grounds are important, for the story which needs to be told is the story of community. All of these individuals share in that story, no matter how brief their time. A high  percentage of those buried in these plots were children who, because they did not live even to the age of five, were robbed of the opportunity to create acts of lasting renown. Many of the others were young men and women in their twenties, cut down in their prime. For great numbers, only fragments of their lives are known, and a few graves bear no identifying mark. Some of those interred accomplished notable feats and were revered

leaders in the Jewish or secular communities, and some may have belonged to extended families that have achieved great public recognition, but it is the lives of all that define the Gold Country pioneer Jewish experience.

I am always curious to figure out what life was like for Jewish men, women, and children during those Gold Rush years. I seek a sense of the whole, piecing together the patterns of family, of religious observance, of social interaction, of commerce. As I walk the cemetery grounds, reading the names on the weathered gravestones, I am struck by this tangible evidence of the early communities, a chapter of the Diaspora set in the American West. These pioneers, often thousands of miles from where they were born, worked within the larger world of the Gold Rush towns to create a new life and culture for themselves and their families. Around me, the worn gravestones demonstrate these Jews' dedication, even in unfamiliar and rugged surroundings, to their faith.

Who are the important people? You will discover this for yourself.

*Susan Morris*

# ❊ A HISTORY ❊

"Gold!"

The January 1848 discovery of gold nuggets in the South Fork of California's American River started a rush to the foothills of the Sierra Nevada that lasted more than two decades. By December 1848, newspapers carrying stories of the great California gold strike reached Jews in communities as distant as New York, Cincinnati, Frankfurt, and the Bavarian town of Winweiler. Letters, guidebooks, and ship advertisements beckoned Jews in Alsace-Lorraine, Posen, Savannah, and New Orleans. The tale of gold for the taking was told and retold in a multitude of languages and on several continents. Jews from many nations and cultures, speaking a variety of languages, joined the thousands of individuals who made the difficult journey to the American West.

The gold fields of that West represented political and social, as well as economic opportunity. Many Jews who fled Europe had lived with restrictions on their freedom to establish businesses, choose a homesite, even to marry. Some had participated in the failed 1848 revolutions and feared for their lives.

Daniel Levy, a French Jew, journalist, and teacher who settled in San Francisco in 1855, wrote: "Among all the areas in the world, California is possibly the one in which the Jews are most widely dispersed. I do not know of one village, one hamlet, one settlement of any kind, either in the North, in the mining area, or the South, the region of ranchos, where they have not established themselves."

As Daniel Levy observed, Jews

Nevada City in the 1850s. From *The Autobiography of Charles Peters.*

Miners working a rocker. From *The Autobiography of Charles Peters.*

populated every region of the mining area. They settled both in the Southern Mines (also known as the Mother Lode), which extends north from Mariposa to Placerville, and in the Northern Mines, which continues in a northerly direction from Placerville to Sierra City.

Life in the mining camps and tent cities was rugged and unpredictable. Death from accident, fire, disease, and primitive medical care was part of the fabric of daily existence. For the Jewish pioneer whose native language and practice of Judaism may have differed from the specific Judaic practices of his neighbor, it was the specter of death that united him with his fellow Jews, impelling them to carry out Jewish law and tradition.

According to Jewish tradition, even before the need for a synagogue, there emerges the need to provide consecrated ground to bury the dead. Daily prayers can be recited and High Holidays, festivals, and marriages celebrated without benefit of clergy, a formal congregation, or a synagogue. However, Jewish law prescribes that the Jew must be laid to rest in consecrated ground. If the deceased has no spouse or child to perform burial rites, it is the responsibility of the entire Jewish community to pray beside the dying, wash the corpse and place it in a shroud, bury the dead with dignity, and pray for the departed soul. Benevolent Societies were traditionally responsible, in the absence of family, for performing these sacred burial rites, and for providing for the welfare of widows and children. Thus, Benevolent Societies were usually the first Jewish organizations formed in the Gold Rush towns.

In the first years of the Gold Rush, the Jewish dead from the predominantly male, makeshift camps and tent cities were often transported to consecrated burial grounds in Stockton or Sacramento. Congregation Ryhim Ahoovim of Stockton (now Temple Israel) and Congregation B'nai Israel of Sacramento were both founded during this period, in 1851. By the mid-1850s, as women and children became part of the growing Gold Rush towns, local burial arrangements became necessary. Smallpox, cholera, and influenza took their toll; fires raged; mining accidents, childbirth, and childhood diseases took life indiscriminately. It became too costly and impractical for communities to bury their dead at distances of as much as fifty or one hundred twenty miles. The establishment of local Jewish cemeteries was an obvious step.

The need for a *minyan,* the ten adult males required by Jewish law to conduct public prayers, including burial rites, often meant many miles of travel to find fellow Jews. For this reason, the Benevolent Societies in the Gold Rush towns often encompassed wide geographic areas.

By the 1850s, businesses began to flourish, and the mining industry evolved from the solitary miner with pick and pan to a more complex organization, using flumes and hydraulic operations. Buildings changed from canvas to wood, then to fireproof brick. Young Jewish males began to marry sometimes with sisters or cousins of their Jewish neighbors and to bring their families to the fledgling communities. Jews lived in multiethnic, multilingual, communities whose residents came from areas as diverse as New England, the American South and Midwest, Italy, Germany, Ireland, France, and China. Of necessity, these Gold Rush towns developed new patterns of integration, and Jews were an integral part of the new communities, joining the Masons, Odd Fellows, fire brigades, political parties, and cultural and charitable organizations.

By the middle of the 1870s, most Jews living in the Gold Rush towns had moved on to the growing urban centers of San Francisco, Sacramento, Oakland, and Los Angeles, where larger populations, transportation improvements, educational opportunities for children, and cultural attractions beckoned. However, that the bulk of Jewish participation in the Gold Rush towns only lasted a few decades in no way diminishes the enduring significance of the Jewish experience in the California Gold Rush.

Many of the leading families who in the late nineteenth century helped create new economic, political, cultural, and educational institutions in the West were Jewish families whose California roots are found in the Gold Country. Among these are such familiar names as Zellerbach, Sutro, Haas, and Levi Strauss. These Jews, as well as the many Jewish pioneers whose names are less renowned, had a part in the establishment of the new culture of the American West.

# SEVEN PIONEER JEWISH CEMETERIES
## ❊ A SELF-GUIDED TOUR ❊

California's Gold Rush towns and communities. Here on consecrated ground are tombstones and burial plots functioning as historical documents that tell us much more than the name and the date of death; here is a testimony to the life of the Jewish Gold Rush pioneer.

## Studying the Gravestones

By studying the inscriptions and carvings on the gravestones, you will discover for yourself the varied patterns of Jewish community life in the Gold Rush towns. Beyond a date of birth or death, you may find mention of a birthplace, a native language, memberships in organizations such as the Masons or Odd Fellows; you may learn about family ties—certainly about the high rate of infant mortality; in a few cases, you may learn of murder.

The style of a gravestone and its carvings may tell you something of the economic status, religious tradition, and aesthetic taste of the deceased—or of his or her survivors. Through the stones and carvings too, you may glimpse the aesthetic preferences of the mid-nineteenth century, the practical issue of availability of materials, and the skills and styles of the carvers.

These gravestones are tangible evidence of the Jews' dedication to their faith even in the remote, rugged Gold Rush towns. Certainly, their worn surfaces demand further research. As you decipher their meaning, patterns emerge; more is

Nestled in the spectacular California Gold Country are seven pioneer Jewish cemeteries, preserved as historic sites and dedicated to the memory of the Jewish Gold Rush pioneers. These six cemeteries are under the trusteeship of the Commission for the Preservation of Pioneer Jewish Cemeteries and Landmarks of the Judah L. Magnes Museum. The Commission was formed in 1963 to rescue these once crumbling and weed-choked historic cemeteries. This guide concentrates on these cemeteries under the Commission's purview.

You will find six of the cemeteries located along State Historic Route 49 in the Gold Rush towns of Sonora, Mokelumne Hill, Jackson, Placerville, Nevada City, and Grass Valley. The seventh Jewish cemetery is located in the Sacramento Delta Gold Rush community of Marysville, once an important supply center for the Northern Mines.

These cemeteries with worn gravestones and poignant inscriptions are tangible evidence that Jews were an integral part of revealed about Jewish community life in the Gold Rush years than appeared at first glance. Your study is revealing more questions than answers.

## A Note on Translations

Most of the stones are carved in two languages, often using Hebrew or Yiddish and English or French. Where two languages appear, translators have often found that each text gives different information. In many cases, the Hebrew or Yiddish words are more descriptive of the life of the individual than is the second language, usually English or French. (Note that Hebrew characters are used both for Hebrew, the language of Jewish prayer, and for Yiddish, a fusion of several European and Slavic languages that is traditionally associated with Eastern European Jews.)

The use of certain words, idioms, and spellings may reflect mid-nineteenth century usage, or merely the literary abilities of the stone-carver or of those who commissioned the stone.

It is curious that none of the stones are inscribed in German, although German was the native tongue of a large percentage of the pioneers. A possible explanation lies in the fact that in Germany it was not until the 1870s, when the modern German state was created, that inscriptions on Jewish gravestones were written in German as well as in Hebrew. The few older Jewish stones in German cemeteries written in German as well as Hebrew indicate a considerable assimilation into the mainstream German community. The use of English, mixed with Hebrew, even on the gravestones of recent immigrants whose English most likely was limited, is another fascinating issue which needs further research.

## Seeking Other Pioneers

The pioneers buried in these cemeteries represent only a fraction of the Jews who participated in the Gold Rush experience. Other Northern California Jewish cemeteries from the Gold Rush era are located in San Francisco, Stockton, and Sacramento. Some California city cemeteries, such as that in Oroville, contain identifiable Jewish sections. Graves of Jewish pioneers may be found in the general areas of many city cemeteries, or in cemeteries under the auspices of the Masons and the Odd Fellows organizations. Many other Gold Rush Jews cannot be found in California cemeteries at all, having returned to their native states or lands when the great rush was over in the 1870s; still other adventurous pioneers followed the rush to the Nevada silver mines, or to the Alaskan gold fields in 1898. Some became famous, most did not, but the lives of all of them are worth exploring, for collectively they define the pioneer Jewish community.

## Solving the Puzzle

Historians are always looking for new pieces of the puzzle to complete the picture of the past. They search for pieces which illuminate the daily lives, issues, and accomplishments of those who paved the way for us. The placement, shape, and style of the Gold Rush gravestones were chosen by the pioneers; they are not the fabrication or embellishment of later generations. They hold a puzzle—a world of puzzles. As you walk along the dirt paths of these pioneer cemeteries, as you read the stones, as you honor the pioneers, perhaps you will find a piece of this world.

Sonora Hebrew Cemetery. Photo: Ira Nowinksi/Judah L. Magnes Museum. Western Jewish History Center.

# ❧ HOW TO USE THIS GUIDE ❧

## Self-Guided Tour

This guide is structured so that you will be able to tour each of the seven pioneer Jewish cemeteries under the trusteeship of the Commission for the Preservation of Pioneer Jewish Cemeteries and Landmarks, as well as Columbia State Historic Park, learning as you go about the men, women, and children who were part of the Jewish experience of the California Gold Rush.

## Easy Reference

Each cemetery has its own chapter, complete with maps, community facts, and brief histories of those interred and of the local Jewish community. A detailed chapter is also devoted to Columbia State Historic Park.

## Maps

Maps provide directions to the cemeteries and for the walking tour of each cemetery site. Numerals in the cemetery plot maps identify the gravestones for the walking tour. Note that these numerals are solely for the purpose of identification and do not reflect a numeric order of burial.

## Number of Gravestones Visible

The number of gravestones cited in each chapter under "Cemetery Facts" refers to the visible stones and not to the number of burials, because definitive information regarding the actual number of burials is not available. It is also quite probable that in each cemetery there are unmarked graves. Where more than one individual is noted on a gravestone, each is listed separately, though the stone is given only one number. Where a mound of earth suggests a grave site, or shards of stone or a base indicate a possible burial, this is noted in the text. In certain instances several gravestones are grouped together, often within a cement plot, and appear to be family groupings. For identification purposes they are identified as family plots, although further research is needed. Several of the grave sites include foot stones, initialed or plain.

## Facts

Much information regarding the pioneer Jewish communities and those interred in the cemeteries comes from the sources listed in the bibliography. I have combined such material with the information actually to be found carved on the gravestones to form a more complete description of the individuals buried in each site.

Remember, however, that for many Jews who were part of the

Marysville Hebrew Cemetery. Photo: Bram Goodwin. Courtesy of Bram Goodwin.

Gold Rush experience, records no longer exist, perhaps never existed. For example, in many cemeteries the total number of burials cited is approximate; there may have been unmarked graves, displaced stones, bodies interred and later moved without any record. (The text will point out these questionable areas.) The search for original source material is ongoing.

### Additional Source Material

*The Jews in the California Gold Rush,* by Robert Levinson, Ph. D. is particularly recommended for those wishing to go into more depth on the subject. This publication and additional reference material on the Jewish experience in the California Gold Rush are given in the bibliography. The Western Jewish History Center of the Judah L. Magnes Museum in Berkeley, California is an important research center and major repository for materials on the Jewish Gold Rush experience.

### Suggested Tour

It is possible to tour a few Gold Country cemeteries on a day trip from the San Francisco Bay Area, Sacramento, Lake Tahoe, or Yosemite. However, to gain an overall understanding of the Jewish experience in the Gold Rush and to get the full flavor of the California Gold Country, more time is recommended. For your convenience, a suggested three-day itinerary is included.

The Gold Country is a popular tourist destination in any season and offers a broad range of lodging, food, and recreational activities for every interest, age, and budget. Although this book does not cover these topics, many fine guides to Gold Country travel are available.

## GENERAL FACTS
### ✳ ABOUT THE ✳
## CEMETERIES

Mokelumne Hill Jewish Cemetery. Gravestone of Abraham Strauss. Photo: Ira Nowinksi/ Judah L. Magnes Museum. Western Jewish History Center.

### Ownership and Current Status

The Commission for the Preservation of Pioneer Jewish Cemeteries and Landmarks of the Judah L. Magnes Museum has title to, and responsibility for the preservation of seven cemeteries under an irrevocable trust. All are designated historic sites and burial is prohibited. Under a nonprofit trusteeship, the Commission took title to these cemeteries for the sole purpose of restoring and overseeing the historic and sacred sites for current and future generations.

### Entry Arrangements

The Sonora, Placerville, Nevada City, Grass Valley and Marysville cemeteries have locked gates. Arrangements must be made prior to your visit to secure entry. For information and access arrangements, please call or write the Western Jewish History Center, Judah L. Magnes Museum, 2911 Russell Street, Berkeley, California 94705, (510) 549-6950. The Museum is open Sunday through Thursday from 10 to 4.

### Cemetery Conditions

Each of the cemeteries is suitable for a walking tour. The Commission makes every effort to provide clean and safe walking paths to make the cemeteries accessible to visitors. However, be advised that the ground is often uneven and, depending on the season, natural vegetation or winter runoff can make walking difficult. In this volume, individual cemetery sections will identify specific conditions, to assist you in planning your tour.

For the benefit of visitors who cannot easily walk the paths, most of the cemeteries can be viewed from outside the gates or fencing. Nevada City cemetery, however, cannot, but requires walking approximately fifty yards from the padlocked gate to the enclosed area containing the gravestones.

*Please keep in mind that each of the cemeteries is consecrated ground. We appreciate your efforts to respect the cemetery, remembering that each gravestone has religious, as well as historical significance. For conservation reasons, please leave preservation and maintenance to those granted authority by the Commission.*

### How to Reach the Commission

If you have questions or comments regarding the cemeteries, or *if you find something which needs immediate attention*, please contact the Commission through the Western Jewish History Center of the Judah L. Magnes Museum at the phone number and address listed above.

If you would like to help preserve these historic and sacred grounds through contribution or membership, please write to the Commission for the Preservation of Pioneer Jewish Cemeteries and Landmarks, c/o Judah L. Magnes Museum, 2911 Russell Street, Berkeley, California 94705.

### Marysville Hebrew Cemetery Restoration

Today's Marysville Hebrew Cemetery is located within the fence that surrounds the Marysville City Cemetery. Since the Commission's founding in 1963, however, it has sought to prove separate ownership, searching for evidence that the once-thriving Marysville Jewish community had followed the pattern of other Jewish communities of the Gold Rush in purchasing its own cemetery land and placing it under the auspices of the Hebrew Benevolent Society. In spring 1994, Marysville postman and historian Dick Marquette found the Marysville Hebrew Benevolent Society's long-sought 1855 recorded deed for purchase of the cemetery land.

December 1994, the Commission filed a petition with the Yuba County Court, Marysville, to be appointed successor trustee to the defunct Marysville Hebrew Benevolent Society. On July 19, 1995 the court granted the Commission the trusteeship. Restoration work may now proceed.

# ❧ READING THE STONES ❧ AND UNDERSTANDING THE TRADITIONS

Jewish burial is a sacred rite that is performed with simplicity and dignity. According to Jewish practice, the body is washed, placed in a shroud, and buried in consecrated ground. If a coffin is used, it is to be of plain wood. Embalming and cremation are not part of Jewish traditional burial rites, nor are flowers at the gravesite. It is considered respectful to the family and the deceased to join the procession to the cemetery and to attend the funeral.

For the observant Jew, it is customary to wash one's hands after visiting a grave and in fact, the Commission is currently looking into various methods to meet this requirement of observant Jews visiting the sites.

According to Jewish custom gravestones face east towards Jerusalem, but for a variety of reasons, including the specific religious customs of the family and a particular cemetery layout, many of the stones in the Gold Country cemeteries face in other directions.

Placing a loose stone on a Jewish tombstone is a custom to indicate that the grave has been visited and the departed remembered.

## *You May Observe Some of the Following Symbols on Stones*

- ◆ Broken tree: life cut off, sometimes interpreted as unexpected death

- ◆ Drooping flower: life cut off in full bloom

- ◆ Candelabra: a woman (in most cases) blessing the Sabbath

- ◆ Hands joined in blessing: the Kohanim, the priestly tribe of Israel

- ◆ Hands holding jugs, or jugs alone: the Levites, who washed the Kohanim's hands before the blessing

- ◆ Hand throwing a coin into an alms box: a philanthropist

- ◆ Hand holding book: a scholar, representing the Jewish interest in learning

- ◆ Year according to the Jewish calendar (e.g. 5610): To find the year of the Gregorian calendar that corresponds to a given Jewish calendar year, subtract 3760 from the Jewish year. Thus, 5610 minus 3760 yields 1850; 5622 minus 3760 yields 1862, etc.

- ◆ Three chains linked: ⚭⚭⚭ Odd Fellows

- ◆ Inverted compass and square: Masonic Order

- ◆ Hebrew Translations:
  פ״נ Here lies buried
  תנצב״ה May his soul be bound up in the bond of everlasting life

## Certain Detective Work Is Often Needed

At times you will need to do detective work to decipher a stone. Consider the gravestones of Kalman and Abraham Strauss in the Mokelumne Hill Cemetery. The dates of burial are given as 1826 and 1828. However, as these dates occurred twenty years before the Gold Rush started, it is a good guess that from some confusion, the inscribed dates take their first half from the Gregorian calendar and their second half from the Jewish calendar years (5626, 5628), that would yield the more likely Gregorian dates of 1866 and 1868.

Unfortunately, too, some stones have been chipped or even toppled during the years and are hard to decipher. In the ennumerated lists of graves for each cemetery, the symbol [?] indicates that the writing on the stone is illegible. And where inscriptions are in Hebrew, scholars inform us that the stonecarvers, or those writing the carvers' instructions, often misspelled words. Further, nineteenth-century written Hebrew differed in some respects from the form used today.

Gravestone of Moses Reeb. Sonora Hebrew Cemetery. Photo: Ira Nowinksi/Judah L. Magnes Museum. Western Jewish History Center.

# ❊ THE STORY OF ❊ TWO JEWISH "FORTY-NINERS"

This is the story of two "forty-niners." About one, Emanuel Linoberg, we know a myriad of things concerning his accomplishments as one of Sonora's leading citizens, and we know as well of his leadership in the early Sonora Jewish community. About the other "forty-niner," seventeen-year-old Hartwig Caro, we know all too little, only that in 1853 young Caro was the first person buried in the Sonora Hebrew Cemetery.

We do know, however, that these two "forty-niners," Linoberg and Caro, shared several things: each walked the dirt streets of the Gold Rush town of Sonora before 1853; each was born in Europe; each was Jewish and each was buried in the 1850s in the Sonora Hebrew Cemetery. Each left behind a grieving family.

Emanuel Linoberg, for whom Sonora's Linoberg Street was named arrived there by early 1849. (This made him truly a "forty-niner," the term used for those who arrived in California before September 9, 1850, the date of its statehood.) Linoberg, a native of Poland, can be described as a man of "firsts." He was elected to Sonora's first town council in 1849, served on the committee to design its first streets, helped found its Masonic Lodge, and participated in some of its first land auctions.

The growing Gold Rush town created a wealth of opportunities for Linoberg. Between 1850 and 1858 he operated businesses in and around Sonora as diverse as: the Quartz Mines and Intelligence Office (a brokerage house for mining claims); a fandango parlor; the Russian Steam Baths, located at the Linoberg Ranch, which catered to miners; and a mule train. His brand, "44," was the first recorded in Tuolumne County. After a raging fire destroyed the town in 1856, Linoberg erected one of Sonora's first fireproof buildings and housed his prosperous mercantile business, Tienda Mexicana, within this stone-and-iron structure.

On December 30, 1851, Linoberg married Pauline Myer in the newly formed Congregation Sherith Israel in San Francisco. (The marriage is recorded in the congregation's first minute book.) Linoberg brought his bride to Sonora, where for many years they would host Jewish weddings and religious gatherings in their home.

In 1856, after an anti-Semitic article appeared in the *Columbia Gazette,* Linoberg wrote a response for the *Sonora Herald* publicly refuting the slur. This exchange was picked up and published in the Philadelphia *Occident,* a Jewish publication with nationwide read-

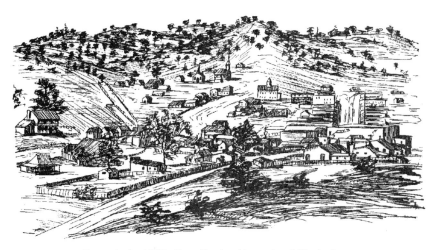

Sonora in the 1850s. From *The Autobiography of Charles Peters.*

ership. Indeed, while Sonora and Columbia may have been newly formed towns in the rugged California interior, they were not isolated from Jewish debate. Newspapers, letters, and merchandise flowed among the Gold Rush towns, the East Coast, and Europe even before the days of the short-lived Pony Express (1860–1861) or the completion of the transcontinental railroad (1869). Jews around the world awaited news of Jewish participants in the Gold Rush; the world was watching California.

In 1857 the Cincinnati *Israelite* published a letter from Linoberg advocating Reform Judaism over Orthodoxy for the Jew in the modern era. Yet, although many Gold Rush Jews favored Reform practices, evidence shows that traditionally observant Jews were also numerous in the Gold Rush communities, particularly in Grass Valley and Nevada City.

Linoberg died in 1858 at the age of forty, leaving Pauline and their two children. He is buried in the Sonora Hebrew Cemetery. His 1856 brick store, later used as a Wells Fargo office, can still be seen at 87 South Washington Street. The few rusted iron letters that remain from the Linoberg name, are visible on the building's south side.

And what of the life of the second "forty-niner," Hartwig Caro? We know so little about this young man who was buried in the Sonora Hebrew Cemetery just three years after California achieved statehood. When did he leave Posen, and why? What route did he take, and how was the journey? What were his hopes, his expectations, his accomplishments? Whom did he leave behind? Did he strike it rich in the gold mines? Did he practice other trades? Why did he die, and who buried him? His tombstone is inscribed "To our beloved son and brother." This inscription is followed by names too faded to read. Did he leave both a mother and father behind, one or several brothers? What happened to them after Hartwig was buried in 1853? Was the Benevolent Society involved in performing the rituals for this young man in his teens? A search of Sonora's historical documents, thus far, has not produced answers to these questions, the same type of questions which might be asked of many buried in these pioneer cemeteries.

Caro's was the first known burial in a Jewish cemetery in the Gold Country, and for that he is noteworthy; however, his simple gravestone, which poignantly illuminates the solitary and precarious life of the adventurer in the California gold fields, stands as a symbol for the many Jewish "forty-niners" who died young and whose graves may now be too faded to read, or the stones crumbled and separated from their foundations.

Each of these stories is important, regardless of what is known about its protagonists' daily life, and accomplishments, for through such accounts, like those of other men, women, and children within this guide book, the Jewish "forty-niner" comes to life.

# SONORA
## ❦ THE COMMUNITY ❦

## Sonora Overview

Sonora is the county seat of Tuolumne County. In 1848 miners from Sonora, Mexico, discovered gold and established a mining community called Sonoranian Camp, later Sonora. A few miles down the road, in what is now Jamestown, was the American Camp.

In 1849, the population of Sonoranian Camp was approximately 5,000, making it one of the Mother Lode's largest mining towns. Violence and racial unrest were a significant part of its early years, and came to a head when the Mexicans were pushed from their claims and forced out after a tax on non-citizen miners was established in 1850. Sonora incorporated in 1851, becoming known as the "Queen of the Southern Mines." Fires swept through the tent and wood town every few years until the advent, in 1856, of brick buildings with iron doors and shutters.

Because of its proximity to the San Joaquin Valley and to the port town of Stockton, Sonora continued, after the Gold Rush, to serve as a commercial and supply center for the Southern Mines. When its placer mining industry ceased, the lumber, agriculture, and cattle industries kept Sonora at the center of the Mother Lode economy.

## Glimpses of the Pioneer Jewish Community

In 1851, the Hebrew Congregation of Sonora was founded. Emanuel Linoberg served as its president for many years. Although the Hebrew Congregation gathered for High Holiday services and other religious observances, no synagogue was ever built. In 1853, under the Congregations's auspices, land was acquired for a cemetery; Hartwig Caro, age seventeen, was the first person buried there.

Sonora's Jewish religious services were held in rented halls and private homes, such as Abraham Barlow's, where it is believed the Torah scroll was kept. According to tradition, the chandelier in

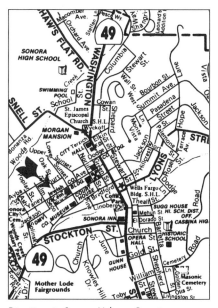

Directions to Sonora Hebrew Cemetery (Yaney Street at Oak): Take Washington Street (Highway 49) to Yaney. Coming from Washington Street, the cemetery is on your left at Oak Street.

Morris Store in Chinese Camp, circa 1890. Photo Archive Collection, Western Jewish History Center.

Sonora's Odd Fellows building was a gift from the Jewish community in exchange for use of the building for High Holiday services. Meyer Baer, a congregation leader, often conducted funeral services and even traveled to San Francisco to purchase twenty to thirty pounds of *matzot* (unleavened bread used during Passover) for the Sonora Jewish community.

The Sonora Hebrew Benevolent Society was founded in 1856, and by 1859 or 1860 it became the Sonora and Columbia Hebrew Benevolent Society. Michael Goldwater (grandfather of former Arizona Senator Barry Goldwater) served for several years as the society's vice-president. In 1860 the combined group gave one hundred dollars for relief of the Jews suffering in Gibraltar—evidence that Jews in the Gold Rush did not isolate themselves from the larger world Jewish community.

According to an old tale, a silver goblet was presented in 1860 to an "F. Hochstein" of Columbia upon his departure for New Orleans, in gratitude for his having conducted religious services in the community. This presentation was reported in the Sonora *Union Democrat* of September 29, 1860. One hundred fifteen years later, this same silver goblet was found and purchased in New York for the Judah L. Magnes Museum, where it is displayed in honor of the Jewish Gold Rush pioneers.

Through the efforts of Julius Baer, the son of pioneer merchant Meyer Baer, the Sonora Hebrew Cemetery continued to be maintained in the twentieth century. Julius died in 1972 at age ninety-six.

## *Jewish Historic Sites*

◆ Baer Store site, 105 S. Washington Street: founded by Meyer Baer in 1851. The Baer Store was in business until 1995.

◆ Linoberg Street: named after Emanuel Linoberg

◆ 87 S. Washington Street: built in 1856 by Emanuel Linoberg, later used as a Wells Fargo office. Look for the Linoberg name on the south side of the building.

## *Worth a Visit*

◆ Tuolumne County Museum and History Center, 158 W. Bradford Avenue, site of the Tuolumne County Historical Society, located within walking distance of the Sonora Hebrew Cemetery.

# SONORA
## ❧ THE CEMETERY ❧

## Cemetery Facts

**Name:** Sonora Hebrew Cemetery
**Founded:** 1853. First Jewish cemetery in the Gold Rush region
**First burial:** 1853
**Last burial:** 1977 (see Ferguson plot notes, below)
**Rededicated as historic site:** January 13, 1974
**Number of gravestones visible:** 43 gravestones, 2 possible burial mounds
**Site characteristics:** Records indicate that a mortuary building may have existed on the cemetery grounds, although no evidence of such a structure exists. The cemetery is enclosed by a stone wall built in the 1850s and is surrounded by Italian cypress trees.
**Special arrangements:** The gate is kept locked. For information and access arrangements, please call or write the Western Jewish History Center, Judah L. Magnes Museum, 2911 Russell Street, Berkeley, California 94705, (510) 549-6950. The Museum is open Sunday through Thursday from 10 to 4.

## Walking Tour

As you walk these paths, you will notice that for some of the individuals buried in these sacred grounds there is much more information in this guide than appears on their gravestone. For others the only information is a gravestone and carved inscription. Sadly, some stones have been too badly damaged to decipher a name; some stones are missing and for some only a foundation or a raised mound of earth remains.

For some individuals we have information from such sources as: recorded deeds and contracts, newspaper articles and advertisements, minute books, diaries, letters, photographs, family histories and family trees, etc. And yet, there are those who shared in the Jewish experience in the California Gold Rush whose lives leave little or no permanent record.

*Upon entering the cemetery, turn to your left and go to the upper row to begin your tour.*

FERGUSON FAMILY PLOT

1.  **Henry Leon Ferguson** (born May 3, 1875, died June 27, 1875).

Sonora Hebrew Cemetery

"Coyle" is carved on the base of the stone.

2. **John Ferguson** (May 7, 1836–February 21, 1903).

   **Rosalie Ferguson** (April 7, 1851–May 29, 1935).

At the top of this gravestone—a relatively new one dating from no earlier than 1936—is an open book, inscribed with the names of John and Rosalie Ferguson, husband and wife. Listed below, on the face of the stone, are the names and the birth and death dates of eight of their twelve children:

> **Infant son** (October 21, 1888–October 30, 1888); **Adele J.** (February 5, 1885–November 25, 1898); **Edna S.** (October 9, 1882–June 20, 1911); **Henry L.** (May 3, 1875–June 27, 1875); **Clara** (April 1, 1877–January 7, 1889); **Charles C.** (October 23, 1886–April 10, 1904); **Carl M.** (January 9, 1881–December 9, 1911); **Frank L.** (January 24, 1891–June 21, 1936).

On the base of the vertical stone is a smaller, separate, and presumably later granite slab inscribed with the names and birth and death dates of four other Ferguson children and/or grandchildren.

> **Benjamin E.** (November 22, 1873–March 26, 1941); **Ruth M.** (July 23, 1894–September 3, 1959); **Grace G.** (June 26, 1892–October 12, 1973); **John A.** (August 2, 1892–July 15, 1977).

A granite marker slab, about two feet from the vertical stone, bears the inscription: "'PA' We finish but to begin. August 2, 1892–July 15, 1977." It appears that John A. Ferguson's family placed the memorial marker after his death in 1977, three years after the cemetery had been dedicated as an historic site and ceased to be used a an active burial ground. It is not known if John A. is buried in the family plot.

The first John Ferguson, proprietor of Gold Mountain Water Co., was a convert to Judaism. He blew the *shofar* (ram's horn) for the High Holidays. In 1873 he married Rosalie Mock in Stockton; her relationship to the Rebecca and Abraham Mock buried in plot 24 is not established, although the age difference might suggest that Rosalie was their daughter.

REEB FAMILY PLOT (1–7)

3. **Moses Reeb** (died 1891, age 56 years).

   **Melanie Reeb** (died 1912).

A native of Germany, Moses Reeb owned a shoe store with his brother. A footstone with "M.R." is at the base of the stone.

A native of France and wife of Moses Reeb, she died in Spokane, Washington.

Moses and Melanie appear on the same stone.

4. **J.C.**

Further identification is unknown.

**5. Louis Cohn.**

The stone is inscribed "Co. C II Inf. Sp. Am. War."

**6. Leah Jacobs** (died 1868, age 11 months).

She was the daughter of Julius and Rosa Jacobs.

**7. Louis Reeb** (1873–1907).

He was the son of Melanie and Moses Reeb. There is a Jacob Leon Reeb in plot 30 and a Jacob Reeb in plot 31. The relationship of either to this family is unknown.

**BAER FAMILY PLOT (8–9)**

**8. Helena Oppenheimer Baer** (July 18, 1840–January 29, 1898).

A native of Stolhofen, Germany, and wife of Meyer Baer, she arrived in Sonora around 1859. She was the sister of Sophie Hannauer, wife of Moses Hannauer, who was a trustee of the Benevolent Society. Meyer Baer leased Hannauer's store in 1852. Helena was the mother of eight children and owned considerable property in her own name.

**Meyer Baer** (1824–1907).

A native of Hamburg, Germany, husband of Helena Baer, he arrived in Sonora in 1851 and became a leader in its Jewish community. He first owned a crockery business, then started a clothing business with a Mr. Leszynsky who moved back to San Francisco in 1852.

Baer's clothing store has continuously been in business since 1851.

**Daisy Gertrude Baer Thayer** (1875–1905, died age 29 years).

She was a daughter of Helena and Meyer Baer.

Helena, Meyer, and Daisy Gertrude Baer are named on the same stone. This large obelisk is flanked by three small individual markers inscribed "Daisy," "Father," and "Mother."

**9. Rebecca Baer** (1872–1946).

The daughter of Helena and Meyer Baer, she was a teacher and ran a popular ice cream and candy store in Sonora.

Gravestone of Helena, Meyer and Daisy Baer. Sonora Hebrew Cemetery. Photo: Ira Nowinski/ Judah L. Magnes Museum. Western Jewish History Center.

Abraham Barlow, late nineteenth century. Sonora. Photo Archive Collection, Western Jewish History Center.

### BARLOW FAMILY PLOT (10)

**10. Abraham Barlow** (1827–1914).

A native of Germany, husband of Emma Barlow, and brother of Hannah Barlow Gumpert (see plot 33), he was a boot and shoe merchant and a leader in the Jewish community.

**Emma Barlow** (1851–1939).

A native of Germany, she was the wife of Abraham Barlow.

**Sylvan Barlow** (1881–1902).

He was the son of Abraham and Emma Barlow.

The Barlow name is carved on the cement steps. There is a solitary marker with the inscribed names Abraham, Emma, and Sylvan.

### WILZINSKI FAMILY PLOT (11–13)

**11. Louis Wilzinski** (1883).

This son of Marie and Max Wilzinski lived one day.

**12. "Mother."**

She was Marie Wilzinski (1866–1918), wife of Max Wilzinski.

**13. "Father."**

He was Max Wilzinski (1847–1921), husband of Marie Wilzinski and owner of a large store in Sonora.

*Return to gate, and begin second row.*

### CLARK FAMILY PLOT (14–15)

Two granite urns mark the entrance to this plot.

**14. Charles Clark** (died 1885, age 60 years).

A native of Delaware County, New York, he was part owner of Big Bonanza Mine.

**15. "Father."**

This solitary stone has the simple inscription "Father." It is possibly G. Joseph, who was a merchant from Canada.

*Return to the gate. The rest of the gravestones are below the central path through the cemetery.*

**16. Hartwig Caro** (1836–1853).

He was native of Posen, Prussia. His was the first known burial in a Jewish cemetery in the Mother

Lode. The Hebrew inscription tells us that he was mourned by a parent and brother, for it says "To our beloved son and brother"; however, the letters which tell us the names of the family he left behind are too faded to read. We do not know if his surviving parent was a mother or father.

### 17. "Daughter of Samuel and Caroline Leon."

This partially restored stone is missing the first name of the child. There is a lamb carved on the stone as well as Hebrew words.

### 18. Henry Cohen (1821–1855).

He was a native of Samosczyn, province of Posen. A wrought iron fence surrounds the grave.

MORRIS AND HARRIS FAMILY PLOT
(19–23)

### 19. Henry Morris (1858–1911, son of James and Pauline Morris).

### 20. Pauline Morris (1904–1905, daughter of Saul and Minnie Morris).

There is a carving of a dove and a decorative scroll on this stone.

### 21. Ida Harris (1863–1916).

Ida's middle (or maiden) name is Morris, as documented on a photograph in the Western Jewish History Center collection. It is not known if Ida was a sister, or perhaps a cousin, to Paul, George, Henry, Saul, and Grace Morris.

**Charles Harris** (1840–1924).

He was most likely the husband of Ida Harris.

### 22. George Morris (1872–1895, son of James and Pauline Morris).

The stone is inscribed "a Martyr to Duty, Native of Cala."

### 23. Pauline Morris (1830–1904).

A native of Prussia, she was the wife of James Morris.

**James Morris** (1825–1885).

He was a native of Mileslaw, Prussia. These stones tell us little, but other facts of this family's history are known. James and Pauline Morris founded a successful and

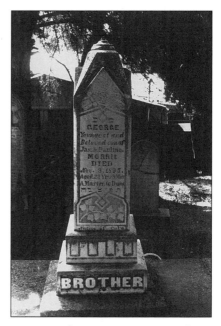

Gravestone of George Morris. Sonora Hebrew Cemetery. Photo: Ira Nowinksi/Judah L. Magnes Museum. Western Jewish History Center.

long running general store in the community of Chinese Camp, several miles south of Sonora on the way to Yosemite. Chinese Camp was established in the first few years of the Gold Rush by Chinese

James Morris, circa 1880. Photo Archive Collection, Western Jewish History Center.

miners driven from their claims in Sonora. The store handled the payroll for the Shawmut Mine and continued in business as long as the mine operated. The Morris family also ran the toll road into Yosemite. James and Pauline had five children: Paul, Henry, George, Saul, and Grace. Paul and Saul Morris ran the Big Oak Flat and Yosemite Stage Company of Chinese Camp. George Morris was murdered in a robbery while protecting the family store, which by 1890 also housed a Wells Fargo

and Company office. An iron shutter from the Morris store, still showing a gaping bullet hole, is part of the Wells Fargo and Company Museum collection.

**24. Rebecca Mock** (1817–1901).

She was a native of France.

**Abraham Mock** (1814–1884).

He was also a native of France.
   Note the Odd Fellows symbol on this stone. In addition, the inscription "1857 B.M.–1930" is found on the base of the stone, possibly referring to a child.

**25. Rose Frindel Davidson**
   (1885–1941, died in Oakland).

**Max Davidson** (1873–1947, businessman).

**26. Mary Jacob** (died August 3, 1862, age 33 years).

She was the wife of Aron Jacob.

**27. Aron Jacob** (died April 4, 1862, age 34 years).

He was a native of Germany, the husband of Mary Jacob, and a Jamestown merchant. According to some records, he may also have been called Albert.
   Notice that both husband and wife died young and a few months apart, suggesting death due to epidemic or perhaps to injuries sustained in one of the town's many fires. All this is speculation, but it gives a glimpse of the precarious nature of the pioneers' daily life. Aron and Mary left a child or children who were sent to San Francisco

to be cared for by relatives, a pattern not uncommon in the Gold Country.

There is a footstone at the base of Aron's grave.

### 28. Unknown grave.

A brick outline of a possible plot is visible.

### 29. Joseph N. Hoffman (1877–1955).

He was a native of Latvia.

### 30. Jacob Leon Reeb (1863–1884).

He was a native of Sonora. No more is known. It is possible that he was the son of Jacob Reeb in plot 31.

### 31. Jacob Reeb (1826–1864).

Here also little is known. He was a native of Germany and, according to the Hebrew inscription, the son of Abraham.

The familial relationship, if any, of the Reebs buried in plots 3, 7, 30, and 31 begs further research. Was Jacob Reeb the older brother of Moses Reeb?

### 32. L. Lippmann (died November 15, 1865).

He was a native of Phalsbourg, France, and this stone is written partially in French. He may be the Louis Lippmann of Columbia who was active in the Odd Fellows there. Note that "Meurthe" is a department in the Alsace-Lorraine region of France; Jews emigrating from France during the period of the Gold Rush were most likely to be from Alsace-Lorraine, for Jews at that time were not allowed to live in other areas of France.

### 33. Hannah Gumpert (died November 28, 1867, age 33 years).

A native of Wittkowo, Prussia, and wife of Elias Gumpert, she was the sister of Abraham Barlow (see plot 10).

The partial standing gravestone with Hebrew inscription, was recently recovered and placed at the gravesite by the Commission. In the early 1960s, Dr. Robert Levinson documented that Hannah's gravestone was inscribed with Hebrew identifying her as the daughter of Rabbi Baruch of Wittkowo. When Hannah and Elias Gumpert were married in Sonora on June 5, 1855, at the Linoberg home, their *ketubah* (Jewish marriage contract) was signed by Emanuel Linoberg, president of the Hebrew Congregation of Sonora, and filed as an official document with the recorder of Tuolumne County. From this contract we learn that Elias Gumpert had sufficient wealth to marry. From the later obituary in the *Hebrew* we discover that Hannah Gumpert was "for many years afflicted with an incurable nervous disorder," that she was the mother of three "interesting" children, and that the Odd Fellows and their wives came to her funeral in great numbers. From other documents it is known that after her death,

Elias, then an officer of the Benevolent Society, moved to Stockton with his children William, Esther, and Bernice, remarried, established a cigar business, and became a prominent member of the Jewish community; after his death he was buried in the pioneer Jewish cemetery of Stockton's Temple Israel.

### 34. Apparent mound.

This may be an unidentified grave.

### 35. Emanuel Linoberg
(1818–1858).

(See Chapter Nine.) Notice the rich carving on this gravestone, indicative of Linoberg's stature in the community. The grieving woman and children suggest untimely death. The Stockton *San Joaquin Republican* reported on March 14, 1858: "Sudden Death. Mr. E. Linoberg, an old resident of Sonora, died very suddenly on Monday last [March 12, 1858, at the age of 40 years], of apoplexy. His funeral was attended by the Masons, Odd Fellows, Hebrew Benevolent Society, Firemen, and a large number of citizens." Pauline, his widow, subsequently married his brother Louis, a resident of Mariposa, a Gold Rush town south of Sonora. Louis was also active in community events, and served as a member of the Bear Valley School Board (in Mariposa) in 1859. In later years, Louis and Pauline moved to San Jose, California, where Pauline owned a millinery business.

Gravestone of Emanuel Linoberg. Sonora Hebrew Cemetery. Photo: Ira Nowinksi/Judah L. Magnes Museum. Western Jewish History Center.

A wrought iron fence surrounds this gravesite.

### 36. David Michael (died February 19, 1858, age 21 years).

He was a native of Fordon, Province of Posen. A fallen leaf adorns the stone.

### 37. An apparent mound.

It may be an unidentified grave. This mound is located, behind David Michael's grave along the west wall.

### 38. Caroline Oppenheimer (1877, died at age 1 month, daughter of Henry and Hannah Oppenheimer).

There is a drooping flower on the stone.

**39. Leon Harris** (1874–1877).

No other identification is known.

**40. Isidor Jacobs** (1862–1869, son of Louis and Rachel Jacobs).

[Note that several graves surrounding Isidor Jacobs, who died at age seven, poignantly demonstrate high rate of infant and child mortality during the Gold Rush years. You only have to look in the immediate vicinity to see the graves of Caroline Oppenheimer, Leon Harris, Fanny Baer, and Jeanette Joseph, all of whom died before their eighth birthday. You will find this tragic pattern in each of the pioneer Jewish cemeteries.]

**41. Felix Edgar Dreyfous** (died October 27, 1855, age 29 years).

He was a native of France, the husband of Catharine Elizabeth Dreyfous, and an auctioneer and merchant. His store was opposite the town's Long Tom Saloon. Another Jewish pioneer, Louis Dreyfuss, native of France and a cousin of the famed French captain Alfred Dreyfus, is buried in the Nevada City Jewish Cemetery, and an infant, Clemence Dreyfus, is buried in the Placerville Jewish Cemetery. It is not known if Felix Dreyfous is related to either of these; however, the variation in spellings does not preclude this possibility.

This elaborately carved gravestone is surrounded by a wrought iron fence. Beneath carvings of an angel, lambs, and a gravestone is the inscription, "To live in hearts we leave behind is not to die. By his wife, Catharine Elizabeth Dreyfous."

**42. Yisrael Ritsvaller** (died and was buried same day May or June, 1863, 4 months and 12 days old, son of Pinchas Ritsvaller).

This stone is written in Hebrew and may have been placed by the Benevolent Society, not the parents, as the stone states, "Here is buried Yisrael, the son of our friend."

**43. Fanny Baer** (died July 5, 1870, age 2 years, daughter of Meyer and Helena Baer).

**44. Jeanette Joseph** (died January 3, 1869, age 3 months, daughter of Harris and Pauline Joseph).

**45. Unidentified grave.**

This repaired stone is inscribed "in memory."

# MOKELUMNE HILL
## ❧ THE COMMUNITY ❧

### *Mokelumne Hill Overview*

Mokelumne Hill in Calaveras County was founded in 1848 and derives its name from a Miwok Indian word meaning "the people of the village Mokel." It is often referred to as Moke Hill. Although now a sleepy town with few businesses, Mokelumne Hill boasted a population of close to ten thousand during the gold strike of 1851.

### *Glimpses of the Pioneer Jewish Community*

The Jewish community in Mokelumne Hill supported both a Hebrew Benevolent Society and a Ladies Hebrew Benevolent Society. However, I.J. Benjamin II, a European chronicler of Jewish life in the West, visited Mokelumne Hill in 1860; he reported that no Jewish organizations existed in the town. And yet, the first burial in the Jewish cemetery had taken place in late December 1859, and so it is possible that Benjamin did not know of these societies, or perhaps the burial occurred before their founding. [I.J. Benjamin's reports are a valuable resource for documentation of Jewish life in the Gold Rush Communities.]

We have scattered information on the members of this Gold Rush community, and as often is the case, the documents which survive, namely deeds and wills, are mostly from the more prominent members of the community. Newspaper articles most often are about prominent citizens, and mostly male. As in all of the Gold Rush Jewish communities, more research is needed to complete the history, revealing the lives of all community members.

The Schweitzer brothers, Bernard and Sam, of Altdorf, Germany ran a store in Mokelumne Hill, later starting a branch in Campo Seco; Bernard had begun his trade in

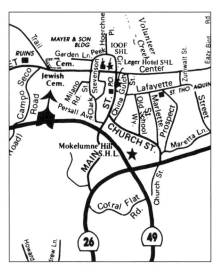

Directions to Mokelumne Hill Jewish Cemetery (Located within the Mokelumne Protestant Cemetery, Center Street): From Highway 49, heading north, take the Historic 49 Mokelumne Hill bypass. Take Main Street to Center Street and turn left. The Jewish cemetery is found at the far end of the larger Protestant cemetery and can be seen from the road, which runs through the cemetery grounds. A wrought-iron fence surrounds this cemetery.

Mokelumne Hill Jewish Cemetery. Strauss family plot. Photo: Ira Nowinksi/ Judah L. Magnes Museum. Western Jewish History Center.

1848 or 1849 as a peddler. Another family, the Gradwohls, were active members of the Mokelumne Hill community, although no Gradwohl is buried in the Jewish cemetery. According to Gradwohl descendents' recollections, Marx Gradwohl, son of Lazare Gradwohl, a German cantor, was considered a community religious leader, and Gradwohl family members from other Gold Rush communities, including distant Grass Valley, would gather in Mokelumne Hill for the High Holidays. In 1863, during the Civil War, Abraham Gradwohl enlisted as a private in the Union Army, Muster Roll, Capt. Hopkins Company Third Brigade, First Division; his brigade served in the western states and territories.

Newspaper articles are the source of much of our information about Mokelumne Hill's Jewish community life. For example, an article in the San Francisco *Weekly Gleaner*, April 11, 1862, states that a circumcision was performed by a visiting *mohel* on the son of Jackson butcher, Kaufman Hexter, a Mokelumne Hill resident. In 1870 the *Weekly Calaveras Chronicle* noted that Mokelumne Hill residents contributed to the newly formed Hebrew Union College in Cincinnati and the San Francisco *Hebrew Observer* recorded donations to the Sanitary Verein, a German club, possibly for use in the Franco-Prussian War.

## Jewish Historic Sites

◆ The stone frame still remains of the L. Mayer & Son store.

## Worth a Visit

◆ Calaveras County Museum and Archives, 30 N. Main Street, San Andreas.

# MOKELUMNE HILL
## ⊯ THE CEMETERY ⊱

## Cemetery Facts

**Name:** Mokelumne Hill Jewish Cemetery
**Founded:** 1859
**First burial:** 1859
**Last burial:** 1878
**Rededicated as historic site:** June 27, 1976
**Number of gravestones visible:** 12
**Site characteristics:** The Mokelumne Hill Jewish Cemetery, although a separate consecrated site, is entered through the Protestant Cemetery. It is located about sixty feet down a dirt path from the main road. The access road is narrow. Not recommended for tour buses.
**Special arrangements:** none

## Walking Tour

As you walk these paths, you will notice that for some of the individuals buried in these sacred grounds there is much more information in this guide than appears on their gravestone. For others the only information is a gravestone and carved inscription. Sadly, some stones have been too badly damaged to decipher a name; some stones are missing and for some only a foundation or a raised mound of earth remains.

For some individuals we have information from such sources as: recorded deeds and contracts, newspaper articles and advertisements, minute books, diaries, letters, photographs, family histories and family trees, etc. And yet, there are those who shared in the Jewish experience in the California Gold Rush whose lives leave little or no permanent record.

*After entering the gate, turn to your right to begin the tour.*

[The fact that many of the gravestones in this cemetery are placed flat on concrete slabs, similar to those in the Grass Valley Jewish cemetery, suggests that this type of placement may have occurred during a restoration of the cemetery.]

1. **David Blum** (1860–1861, infant son of Isaac and Harriet Blum).

2. **Caroline Davidson** (1859–1861, daughter of Louis and Manchen Davidson). There was a Samuel Davidson listed as a peddler in the *Great Register*, a register of voters,

Mokelumne Hill Jewish Cemetery

from 1866, who may have been a relation.

3. **Michael Abel** (died January 24, 1868, age fifty years).

According to historian Robert Levinson, Abel, who was a native of Prussia and a clothing store owner, had inventory appraised for his estate in excess of $2,400, which included calf boots from $2.50 to $4.00 and black frock coats at $12.00 apiece.

4. **Rachel Abel** (died May 5, 1863, age forty-five years, wife of Michael Abel).

5. **Unknown grave.**

A base for a gravestone exists, with no identification.

6. **Unknown grave.**

This stone, directly in front of the gate, is inscribed "E.J." No further identity is known.

7. **Isidor Sokolowski** (died December 26, 1870, age 57 years).

A native of Prussia, he was the husband of Pauline Furst Sokolowski, the sister of Herman Furst of Oakland. After Isidor's death, Pauline moved back to Oakland. A footstone is at the base.

8. **Adolf Kroft** [possibly Kraft] (1851–1860).

There is a carving of broken leaves on this stone.

9. **Isaac Lurch** (1831–1859).

Originally from Upper Rhenish, Bavaria, he was for a time a resident of Wilmington, North Carolina, and after 1855 a citizen of Lancha Plana, a Gold Rush community south of Mokelumne Hill. Lurch's burial was the first in the Mokelumne Hill Jewish Cemetery; the fact that he lived a good distance from the town supports the view that the Jewish community had a wide geographic base. Lurch was an active member of the Masons; the intricately carved relief under the Hebrew lettering on his stone represents the Masonic funeral service. San Francisco's *Weekly Gleaner* reported: "He was buried last Friday morning, Dec. 30, at Mokelumne Hill, in the Jewish burying ground. His remains were accompanied by the Masonic and Odd Fellow's fraternities of Amador and Calaveras counties, also by the firemen of Lancha Plana. The funeral procession which was headed by a band of music, ordered by the Masonic

Gravestone of Isaac Lurch. Mokelumne Hill Jewish Cemetery. Photo: Ira Nowinksi/Judah L. Magnes Museum. Western Jewish History Center.

members, numbered over 500 persons, among whom were the Jewish ladies of Mokelumne Hill, was the largest that ever took place in this part of the country. The deceased leaves an aged mother, and two sisters, whose sole support he was, to mourn his loss."

A footstone is at the base.

The next three gravestones are surrounded by a wrought iron fence and contain the Strauss and Strouse gravestones. The reason for the difference in spelling between the mother's and the sons' inscriptions is unknown.

STRAUSS FAMILY PLOT (10–12)

**10. Abraham Strauss** (son of Moses Strauss).

As on Kalman Strauss' stone, the Hebrew date of death, 5629, is most likely correct, and the corresponding Gregorian date should be October 1868, not 1828 as inscribed. (Since the date of death is in October, the autumnal Jewish New Year probably accounts for the residual apparent one-year discrepancy).

"Shafer & Co. Jackson" appears on the bottom right of the stone. It is interesting to note that the words "Shafer and Company" appear on the Royal Brown gravestone in the Marysville Hebrew Cemetery. Brown died in 1871. At the time the book went to press, no information was available about this stonemasonry firm. Subsequent research regarding Shafer & Co. and other stonecutting firms may reveal the needed information the Jewish pioneers' decisions concerning gravestone design, wording, and ornamentation.

**11. Kalman Strauss** (son of Moses Strauss).

The stone gives the Hebrew date of death as 5626 and the corresponding Gregorian date as May 1826. This discrepancy might be a carving mistake, as it appears unlikely that the Strauss brothers were in Mokelumne Hill in 1826. The corresponding date to the Hebrew year 5626 is 1866, a date of death which, like that of 1868 for Abraham (below), seems more probable.

Another interesting fact is that the inscription reads "He died the 9th and was buried the 15th day of Sivan." This six-day delay in burial is contrary to Jewish custom. Was Kalman far from Mokelumne Hill when he died?

**12. Bertha Strouse** (1799–1878, wife of Moses Strouse).

She was a native of Sterndorf, Germany and died in Virginia City, Nevada.

The haunting question remains: Why the difference in spelling of this mother's last name from that of her sons?

# JACKSON
## ❧ THE COMMUNITY ❧

## *Jackson Overview*

The county seat of Amador County, Jackson was founded in 1848. It was not known for its placer mining activities, although it served as a supply and social center for the early mines. However, in the latter part of the nineteenth century, Jackson attracted corporate mining interests and gained national renown for two hardrock, deep-shaft mines, the Kennedy and the Argonaut. Large-scale mining operations continued until World War II; the giant head-frames of the Kennedy Mine Tailings Wheels still stand as evidence of early twentieth-century environmental mining standards, for the large wheels were constructed to keep the mountain streams free of mining waste. Jackson remained a major mining center longer than any other Gold Rush town in the Southern Mines. (In the Northern Mines region, Grass Valley and Nevada City re-mained viable mining centers with large corporate operations well into the twentieth century.) During the hardrock mining years, Jackson had the reputation of a bawdy, open town, welcoming the lonely miner.

## *Glimpses of the Pioneer Jewish Community*

Existing records do not show evidence of a Hebrew Benevolent Society in Jackson. However, the community formed the B'nai Israel Congregation in 1857 and built one of only two synagogue buildings in the Gold Rush area, the other being in Placerville. It is a curious fact that a few references to Jackson's synagogue list its name as Beth Israel. B'nai Israel's constitution and by-laws specify, "The religious service in the Synagogue of this Congregation shall be according to *Minhag Polen*," the Polish order of service.

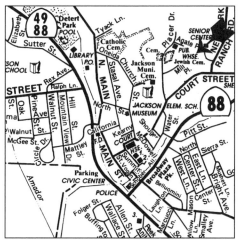

Directions to Givoth Olam (Cemetery Road off Placer): From Highway 49, enter Jackson on North Main Street. Turn right on North Main; bear left on Main at the National Hotel, and continue on Main until it becomes Water Street. Continue on Water to Placer, turn left onto Placer and then take another left on Cemetery Road. Take Cemetery Lane to its end. Givoth Olam Cemetery, lined by Italian cypress trees, is on your right. The gate is reached up a private road. Note the Jackson City Cemetery on the left side of Cemetery Lane.

This 1894 painting by Ivy Mace Yarrington depicts Jackson circa 1880. The likely former site of the B'nai Israel synagogue can be found by locating the last of three small houses to the left of the large schoolhouse with the flag. Courtesy of the Amador County Museum.

On September 12, 1857, a notice of B'nai Israel's dedication appeared in the *Amador Dispatch* "The Israelites of Jackson and surrounding towns are respectfully notified that the Synagogue at Jackson is completed, and they are requested to meet there on Friday, the 18th of September [New Year's Day] for the purpose of devine [sic] worship." Jackson merchant Mark Levinsky was the first president of B'nai Israel; his brother and business partner John was the second. An 1886 advertisement in the local paper read, "The Levinsky Brothers would respectfully inform their customers that the store will be closed on September 10 and 11, and the 19th, on account of the holidays."

During the holidays, Jews from surrounding communities such as Mokelumne Hill, Sutter Creek, Volcano, El Dorado, and Placerville were often asked to help officiate at the services. I.J. Benjamin II, the European wanderer and chronicler, noted in 1860 that there were thirty-five Jews in Jackson, and regretted that, although they had a building, they had no Torah but, rather, borrowed one from San Francisco. B'nai Israel, the wooden synagogue built on Church Street next to the brick public schoolhouse, was by 1869 no longer used for services, perhaps because the congregation had outgrown the facility. After 1869, the congregation met in Jackson's Masonic Hall; the synagogue building was used as a school until 1888.

### An Historical Note

It is interesting to note that by 1850, after the first Jewish High Holiday service in the West was held in 1849 in San Francisco in a tent on Jackson and Stockton Streets, that city's Jews had split into two congregations, Sherith Israel and Emanu-El, to accommodate differences in the *minhag*, the order of prayer for the services. Congregation Emanu-El followed a German tradition and Congregation Sherith Israel followed the Polish *minhag*; as noted above, Jackson's Congregation B'nai Israel's Constitution also specified the Polish *minhag*. Could there have been an actual connection between Congregation Sherith Israel of San Francisco and Congregation B'nai Israel of Jackson? Both congregations named their cemeteries Givoth Olam, Hills of Eternity. Documentation does not give clear evidence of an overt relationship between the congregations, however; perhaps familial ties and shared culture created similar institutions in the two communities. Sacramento's Congregation B'nai Israel was founded in 1851, and it is certainly possible that there was a direct tie between the Sacramento and Jackson congregations. Here is an interesting case where documentation has not been located to confirm this enticing and interesting theory.

It should be mentioned that Jackson's *Amador Dispatch* contained advertisements and articles that demonstrated a constant interaction between the Jackson and San Francisco Jewish communities. The Levinsky brothers advertised that a family member in San Francisco was receiving new shipments of goods from New York and Europe. (This may have been their brother Louis, who had once operated a gold mine in Amador County.) And San Francisco congregations solicited funds for their buildings and charities from fellow Jews in "the interior," the term regularly used for the Gold Rush areas.

## Jewish Historic Sites

◆ Plaque on the site of B'nai Israel. California Registered Historical Landmark No. 865 at Church and North Streets, next to Jackson Elementary School.

## Worth a Visit

◆ Amador County Museum, 225 Church Street

◆ Kennedy Tailings Wheels, Jackson Gate Road

## Cemetery Facts

**Name:** Givoth Olam (Hills of Eternity)
**Founded:** 1857
**First burial:** 1857
**Last burial:** 1921
**Rededicated as historic site:**
June 27, 1976
**Number of gravestones visible:** 32
**Site characteristics:** Cemetery is surrounded by cypress trees and a wrought iron fence.
**Special arrangements:** none

## Walking Tour

As you walk these paths, you will notice that for some of the individuals buried in these sacred grounds there is much more information in this guide than appears on their gravestone. For others the only information is a gravestone and carved inscription. Sadly, some stones have been too badly damaged to decipher a name; some stones are missing and for some only a foundation or a raised mound of earth remains.

For some individuals we have information from such sources as: recorded deeds and contracts, newspaper articles and advertisements, minute books, diaries, letters, photographs, family histories and family trees, etc. And yet, there are those who shared in the Jewish experience in the California Gold Rush whose lives leave little or no permanent record.

*After entering the cemetery, turn right to begin your tour.*

1.  **Rachel Levinsky** (stillborn, 1857, daughter of Mark and Fanny Levinsky).

Mark Levinsky, active in the Masons, was senior warden of Amador Lodge No. 65 and an officer in the Sutter Arch Masons. A drooping flower adorns the stone. A footstone is between the base of stones one and two.

2.  **Alphonse Levinsky** (1861, three days old, son of Mark and Fanny Levinsky).

There is a faded drooping rose on the stone.

3.  **Abraham Levinsky** (stillborn, October 13, 1862, son of Mark and Fanny Levinsky).

```
1 2 3 4 5    6 7 8      11        18 19 20
                        13 14 15 16    21 22
            9    10        12    17        23

                                    24 25




               29 28 27
   32 31 30            26
            CEMETERY LANE
```

Givoth Olam Cemetery, Jackson

4. **Harriette Olga Levinsky** (1858–1860, daughter of John and Mathilda Levinsky).

John Levinsky, the dry goods business partner of his brother Mark Levinsky, left Jackson in 1858 to search for gold along Canada's Fraser River.

5. **Edith Rachel Levinsky** (stillborn, January 28, 1863, daughter of J. and M. Levinsky).

6. **Hannah Samuels** (1863–1867).

7. **Rosa Samuels** (1867–1868).

8. **Hyman Samuels** (1873–1877, son of Joseph and Susan Samuels).

A kneeling lamb is carved on the stone.

9. **Mariam Cohn** (1797–1882, mother of Susan Samuels).

She was a native of Prussia.

10. **Samuel M. Samuels** (died 1877, son of Joseph and Susan Samuels).

There is a kneeling lamb on the stone.

11. **Aron Weil** (died 1921, age 87 years).

Weil served as a trial juror in 1868. His daughter Gennetta is listed on the same stone, which is surrounded by a wrought iron fence.

> **Gennetta Weil** (1866–1869, daughter of A. and E. Weil).

12. **Abie Peiser** (1870–1877, son of I. and P. Peiser).

There is a footstone inscribed "A.P."

13. **Isaac Peiser** (died 1877, age 32 years).

Peiser was a native of Peiseru, Russia.

14. **John von Peiser** (1871, age 2 months, son of T. and P. Peiser).

15. **Julius Peiser** (1854–1894).

16. **Small broken headstone with initials "J.N.," "L.N.," "A.N."**

No further identity is known.

17. **Rose Newman** (died 1877, age 1 year, 10 months, 16 days).

STECKLER FAMILY PLOT (18–20)

18. **Caroline Steckler** (1834–1860, wife of Charles Steckler).

A native of Furth, Bavaria, she most likely was the second wife of Charles Steckler. His first wife, Hette, is buried in grave 20.

19. **Charles Steckler** (1824–1880).

A native of Bohemia, he owned several business ventures in Jackson and surrounding communities: a grocery business in Jackson with Moses Brumel and P. Vertimer, which lasted until 1858, and saloons in Volcano and Jackson. Steckler later ran a dry-goods store, where his advertisement stated "I sell Cheap for Cash Only." He was a member of the Masons and the Odd Fellows, as indicated by the carved symbols on his stone.

**20. Hette Steckler** (died 1858).

A native of Rogasen, Prussia, she was the first wife of Charles Steckler.

GOLDNER FAMILY PLOT (21–25)

A large red marble marker inscribed "Goldner" denotes this large family plot. It appears that this stone does not mark a gravesite.

**21. Rosalia Goldner** (died 1881, age 42 years).

A native of Prussia and the sister of Rachel Haines, she is buried in the Goldner plot. Rosalia was twenty-six at the time she hosted Rachel's wedding at her home, twenty-nine when she buried that sister.

**22. Herman Goldner** (died 1906, age 79 years, husband of Rosalia).

A native of Prussia, he owned a variety store in Jackson. From 1885 to 1889 he was U.S. Postmaster in Jackson, and from 1882 to 1884 and 1890 to 1906, he was the town's Justice of the Peace.

**23. Rachel Haines** (died 1868, age 24 years, wife of A. Haines).

Rachel Hoffman Haines, a native of Prussia, came to Jackson from Germany to be with her sister, Rosalia Hoffman Goldner. Rachel and Abraham Haines were married in the Goldner home in Jackson on November 5, 1865, when Rachel was twenty-one years old.

The Hebrew inscription on Rachel's stone gives the Haines name as Hahn. From other sources we know that Rachel Haines' husband, Abraham (Abe) Haines, a native of Germany, was one of many Haines brothers to emigrate to California in the 1850s and 1860s. Abraham's uncle, George Haines, was active in the Sacramento Jewish community, and a relative, Gabriel Haines (possibly the same person as George), was a spokesperson for the Jewish community in the California legislature against the repressive Stowe bill, which would have limited trading on Sundays. Representative Stowe attacked Jews as "undesirable citizens."

Wedding invitation of Abraham Haines and Rachel Hoffman, Jackson, 1865. Courtesy of Lorraine and Bob Guggenheim.

Sutter Creek. Wedding photograph of Abraham Haines, 1865. Courtesy of Lorraine and Bob Guggenheim.

Abe and Rachel Haines lived in El Dorado, a few miles from Placerville, where Abe was a member of the Cemetery Association, which formed the Shaareh Shomayim (Gates of Heaven) Cemetery of El Dorado; however, when Rachel Haines, the first Jewish resident of El Dorado to die, was buried, she was interred in her sister's family plot. Subsequently, Abe Haines left the Gold Country, married Hulda Levison, from Strasburg West Prussia, in 1871, and moved to Yolo County in the Sacramento Valley, opening a store in Madison. Allie Haines, Abe's son, later owned the Summerfield and Haines clothing store on Market Street in San Francisco until his death in 1959. The Haines and Goldner families continued their close relationship.

**24. Alfred** (died October 10, 1910).

He was a native of California.

**25. Robert** (died December 25, 1924).

He was a native of California.

**26. Jacob Fabien** (born March 16, 1862, died April 4, 1862, son of Abraham Myer Fabien).

**27. Benjamin Baker** (1845–1859).

A flower is carved on the stone. Nothing else is known to us.

**28. David Danielewicz** (1860–1872, son of Gustav and Jettle Danielewicz.).

He was born in Mokelumne Hill and died in Sutter Creek. This stone is in the shape of an obelisk.

**29. Kalonymos ben Natan.**

This inscription is entirely in Hebrew, which tells us that "we are crying about" Kalonymos, the son of Nathan who died on the 19th and was buried on the 20th of February 1878.

**30. Odell Isaacs** (died 1879, age 4 months).

Were these three Isaacs children felled in epidemics? What were they like? We do not know.

**31. Beatrix Isaacs** (died 1883, age 1 year, daughter of M. and Mary Isaacs).

**32. Bernice Isaacs** (died 1884, age 8 years, daughter of M. and Mary Isaacs).

There is a faded six-line verse on this stone.

# PLACERVILLE
## ❦ THE COMMUNITY ❦

## Placerville Overview

The county seat of El Dorado County, Placerville, in close proximity to the Coloma gold discovery site, has had several names. It was originally called Dry Diggings because miners needed to haul their dirt-covered finds to running water to test for gold. Soon, however, it earned the nickname Hangtown, from the hanging tree on the main street, which was used for swift, though perhaps not always blind, justice. The town once had the third largest population in California, surpassed only by San Francisco and Sacramento, and was incorporated in 1854 under the name of Placerville. Early in the Gold Rush, Placerville was the final stop on the long Overland Trail; in 1860 it became a stop for the short-lived Pony Express. When the gold ran out, Placerville became an important stop in the Comstock Nevada silver rush, this time marking the beginning of a trail heading *east* to riches.

## Glimpses of the Pioneer Jewish Community

In 1854 the Placerville Hebrew Benevolent Society was founded and purchased land for its cemetery. A Ladies Hebrew Benevolent Society was also formed. In 1856 Marcus Abraham of nearby Grizzly Flat was the first person buried in the cemetery.

In 1861, Congregation B'nai B'rith, formed under the auspices of the Placerville Hebrew Benevolent Society, erected a synagogue on the corner of Cottage and El Dorado Streets. In 1878, after a storm destroyed this first building, a second synagogue was constructed on the south side of Mill Street (now Spring Street); it was abandoned and the land sold in 1903, with Michael Simon acting as the sole remaining Trustee of the Hebrew Benevolent Society in the sale.

Henry Greenberg, a native of Huttenbach, Bavaria, was the first president of Placerville's Hebrew Benevolent Society; however, he and his wife Marie left Placerville in the late 1850s to settle in San

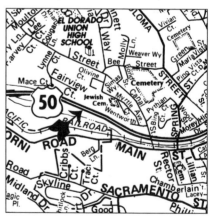

Directions to Placerville Jewish Cemetery (Myrtle and Myrtle Lane): Take Highway 50 (west from 49) to Canal Street. Go left on Wentworth, then right on Myrtle. Proceed up Myrtle. The cemetery is on your left at the corner of Myrtle and Myrtle Court.

Francisco, where he served as a director of a similar Jewish institution, San Francisco's Eureka Benevolent Society.

Doctor Samuel Snow was also an original member of the Hebrew Benevolent Society. He had arrived in California in August 1850, leading a wagon train from Council Bluffs, Iowa. With him were his German Catholic wife Paulina, her parents, and the Snows' infant son Emanuel, born under a wagon during the journey. The doctor established land rights on the site of the future state capital in Sacramento, but lost the land when he went to examine mining conditions in Placerville and his family packed up and left their plot to join him. Samuel Snow became a key participant in the economy of Placerville and the nearby camps of Iowaville and Dogtown, selling mining supplies, running a hotel and restaurant, and practicing medicine. The Snow family continued their business investments in ranching, lumber, and mining for many generations; Snows Road in Placerville is named for them.

The interesting history of Placerville's Round Tent Store on Main Street reveals a succession of Jewish owners during the Gold Rush years and into the early twentieth century. Records show that in 1853 Caroline Tannenwald of Cincinnati paid eight thousand dollars for the store. (Women could own property in their own name according to an 1852 California

Placerville, circa 1860. Lazarus and Caroline Tannenwald. Courtesy of Betsy Klein Schwartz.

statute.) Henry Greenberg also was said to have been an owner of the store in the early 1850s, though a deed bearing his name has not been uncovered. When the original wood and canvas frame was destroyed in the 1856 fire, the store was rebuilt in brick, with its signature rounded front kept intact. Caroline Tannenwald sold the Round Tent Store to fellow Cincinnatian Aaron Kahn in 1853; subsequently Michael Simon bought it. The Round Tent Store is still in existence on Placerville's Main Street today, though no longer canvas covered nor boasting a rounded front.

One of the store's owners, Aaron Kahn, was a merchant in clothing and gold dust and an active member of Jewish and secular Placerville in the 1860s. He served as president of the Hebrew

Benevolent Society, officer in the Masons, and treasurer of the fire department; in 1865 Kahn was elected to the Board of Delegates of the National Israelites. Aaron Kahn and his wife, Mathilda Hilp Kahn, had two children, who were born in Placerville.

Several other members of the Placerville Jewish Community originated from Cincinnati, home to many German Jewish immigrants. Records show that Caroline Tannenwald's husband, Lazarus, sold his seats in KK [Kal Kodesh] Bene Israel, Cincinnati, in 1849 and brought a *Sefer Torah* from Cincinnati to San Francisco's Congregation Emanu-El in the early 1850s. The Tannenwalds bought and sold much property in Placerville before returning to Cincinnati. The 1853 purchase of the Round Tent Store, however, was only in Caroline's name. Merchant Henry Raphael was a member of the Democratic Committee, an officer in the Masons, and a grand jury member; like Kahn, he later returned to Cincinnati. Research shows that the Kahn, Raphael, and Tannenwald families were connected through kinship and business activities. Another prominent Jewish

Placerville, circa 1860. Henry Raphael. Courtesy of Betsy Klein Schwartz.

merchant and property owner, Abraham Seligman, who was to emigrate to New York by 1864 to form the investment firm J. and W. Seligman and Co., was a member of the *E Clampus Vitus*, an organization which parodied the ritual and solemnity of the popular fraternal orders of the day.

In nearby El Dorado and Diamond Springs several merchants in 1865 formed the Shaareh Shomayim (Gates of Heaven) Association and later built a cemetery. Abraham Haines was a member of this association (see Rachel Haines, Jackson Cemetery section above). It is believed that, at the turn of the century, that all the bodies from the Shaareh Shomayim Cemetery were disinterred and taken to San Francisco for reburial in Jewish cemeteries.

## Jewish Historic Sites

◆ Site of first synagogue, B'nai B'rith, at Cottage and El Dorado Streets

◆ Round Tent Store, 326 Main Street

## Worth a Visit

◆ El Dorado County Museum, 100 Placerville Drive

◆ Main Street Historic Area

# PLACERVILLE
## ⋘ THE CEMETERY ⋙

## Cemetery Facts

**Name:** Placerville Jewish Cemetery
**Founded:** 1854
**First burial:** 1856
**Last burial:** 1968
**Rededicated as historic site:**
January 26, 1964. The *E Clampus Vitus* organization assisted in the rededication ceremonies and had worked to assure the site's preservation as an historic site.
**Number of gravestones visible: 22**
**Site characteristics:** Cemetery is surrounded by a fence and is in a residential area.
**Special arrangements:** There is a padlocked gate. For information and access arrangements, please call or write the Western Jewish History Center, Judah L. Magnes Museum, 2911 Russell Street, Berkeley, California 94705, (510) 549-6950. The Museum is open Sunday through Thursday from 10 to 4.

## Walking Tour

As you walk these paths, you will notice that for some of the individuals buried in these sacred grounds there is much more information in this guide than appears on their gravestone. For others the only information is a gravestone and carved inscription. Sadly, some stones have been too badly dam-

aged to decipher a name; some stones are missing and for some only a foundation or a raised mound of earth remains.

For some individuals we have information from such sources as: recorded deeds and contracts, newspaper articles and advertisements, minute books, diaries, letters, photographs, family histories and family trees, etc. And yet, there are those who shared in the Jewish experience in the California Gold Rush whose lives leave little or no permanent record.

*Upon entering the cemetery, turn to your right to begin your tour.*

**1. Marcus Abraham** (1822–1856).
A native of Nakel Province, Posen, he was a resident of Grizzly Flat and the first person to be buried in the cemetery. Abraham was a merchant, and records of his estate recorded a clothing inventory, valued at $1,845, that included men's and women's clothing, fancy goods, and mining outfits.

Placerville Jewish Cemetery

Documents show that Abraham was generous with credit and was "Lamented by his numerous friends, who deplore his premature departure."

2. **Clemence Dreyfus** (1862, age 6 months).

This stone has a drooping flower.

3. **Sarah Lewis** (died 1861, daughter of Henry and Pauline Lewis).

Her mother, Pauline Lewis, is buried in plot 8.

4. **Ernestein Cahn** ("of D[iamond] Spring").

No more is known.

5. **Charlotte Mierson** (died 1875, age 2 years, 10 months, 19 days, daughter of Augustus and Emma Mierson).

Augustus Mierson, with his brother-in-law Godfrey Jewell, ran a clothing business that became the Mierson Banking Company, later A. Mierson and Sons; in 1919 Augustus's son Max reorganized the bank which was later sold to the Bank of America. In the mid-1860s, Augustus served on the El Dorado County grand jury.

6. **David Simon** (1852–1917).

He was possibly the husband of Sarah Simon and the father of Jeanette Simon, buried in plot 14. However, we do not yet know. There is a Masonic symbol on the stone.

7. **"Simon."**

This is simply a large stone with the single word "Simon." The Simon family, with roots in Rogasen, Germany, lived in Placerville for many generations.

Michael Simon was a trustee of the Hebrew Benevolent Society in 1878, when it sold the land on which Placerville's first synagogue had stood; he acted as the surviving trustee when the second synagogue's land was sold. He was also among the succession of Jews to own the Round Tent Store.

Albert Simon was mayor of Placerville in 1924–1928; the town's Simon Drive was named after him. He is buried in the Placerville City Cemetery.

8. **Pauline Lewis** (died January 1858).

She was the wife of Henry Lewis. Pauline and Henry donated the Mill Street property used for the second synagogue. It is even possible that Henry Lewis conducted services for the synagogue and is referred to in newspapers as L. Lewis. Pauline was the mother of Sarah, buried in plot 3.

9. **Edward Cohn** (1832–1880).

He was a native of Exin, Germany. His wife's name is unknown. The stone carving depicts hands raised in blessing, the symbol for the Kohanim.

10. **Herman Landecker** (1874–1877).

Gravestone of Herman Landecker. Placerville Jewish Cemetery. Photo: Ira Nowinksi/ Judah L. Magnes Museum. Western Jewish History Center.

Crossed ferns are elaborately carved on the stone, but we have no information on this child's family.

**11. Abraham Simon** (1854–1869).

His possible relationship to Michael or David Simon (see plot 7), or their relations, is not known.

**12. Edmond Haas** (1864, age 2 months).

  **Lucien Jacob Haas** (1863, age 5 months).

These infants' parents were Abraham and Henriette Haas.

**13. Nelson Haas** (1853–1858, born in Placerville).

It is possible that he was related to the Haas children buried in plot 12.

**14. Jeanette Simon** (died June 21, 1891, age 1 year, 7 months, daughter of David and Sarah Simon).

**15. Jacob Kohn** (1818–1902, husband of Theresa Kohn).

He fled his native Hungary after the failure of the 1848 revolution there, and arrived in El Dorado County in 1849. He first prospected the mines near Beaverton and later engaged in business in Placerville. Coon Hollow Road is said to be named for him.

**16. Theresa Kohn** (1830–1892, wife of Jacob Kohn).

SNOW FAMILY PLOT (17–21)

**17. Joseph Snow** (1851–1926, son of Samuel and Paulina Snow).

He engaged in mining and cattle raising, using the brand "SS" in honor of his father.

**18. Samuel S. Snow** (1818–1892).

A native of Germany, he was the husband of Paulina Snow. (See the Snow family story in "Glimpses of the pioneer Jewish community," above.) The stone has clasped hands carved beneath Snow's name.

**19. Paulina Snow** (1827–1882, "wife of Susmon Snow").

The stone shows a dove with an olive branch in its mouth. Paulina is the wife of Samuel S. Snow; it is not known why "Susmon" is used instead of "Samuel."

**20. Herman Snow** (1861–1932).

**21. Charles Snow** (1868–1932).

**22. George Yohalem** (1895–1968).

This stone shows an open book framed with roses. We know only the dates for this person, as for so many of those buried in here.

# NEVADA CITY
## ❧ THE COMMUNITY ❧

## *Nevada City Overview*

The seat of Nevada County, Nevada City earned its name, *nevada*, Spanish for snowfall, after a fierce snow storm blanketed the area in 1850. At first simply called Nevada, it later added "City" to avoid confusion with the newly admitted state, some sixty miles to the north. In the early years, miners utilized placer mining techniques, using pans, flumes, and sluice boxes. However, the creeks around Nevada City would dry up during the summer months, halting the mining process, and, as early as 1852, inventive miners created a method to transport water with the force of a running river to their claims in order to continue their work. This new method, called hydraulic mining, used large cannon-type implements to wash away hillsides to get at the gold-bearing rock. The Malakoff Diggins, one of the world's largest hydraulic mines, operated until this environmentally destructive technique was outlawed in 1920.

Throughout the late nineteenth and early twentieth centuries, hardrock mining continued in the Nevada City and Grass Valley areas, with many pioneers of Cornish descent coming to Nevada City and Grass Valley to work the mines.

## *Glimpses of the Pioneer Jewish Community*

Nevada City and Grass Valley are but four miles apart, yet, during the Gold Rush decades, each maintained its own Jewish organizations. Unlike the Jewish Benevolent Societies of Sonora and Columbia, which combined in 1860, the Nevada City and Grass Valley groups did not merge. Each community supported one or two Jewish religious, social, or fraternal organizations, and each bought land and built a cemetery and probably adjacent mortuaries.

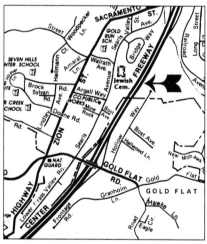

Directions to Nevada City Jewish Cemetery (Searls Avenue near Walwrath): Heading north on Highway 49/20, take Gold Flat Road, Ridge Road. Turn left, onto the freeway overpass. Then take an immediate right onto Searls Avenue, which parallels the freeway. Proceed on Searls for four-tenths of a mile. The entrance to the cemetery is an unmarked private driveway on your right with a "No Trespassing" sign. Walwrath Avenue is on your left, just a bit beyond the cemetery driveway. (If you reach Gold Run Elementary School, you've gone too far.) Proceed down the driveway and park on the right, in front of the cemetery gate.

Records show, however, that some individuals belonged at times to organizations in both cities.

One possible explanation for the success of two separate Jewish communities in such close proximity is that a large percentage of the Jewish population of Grass Valley consisted of single males, even after 1855, when Jewish women became a larger proportion of the population. It is speculated that these bachelors, who often resided in hotels and boarding houses, supported and needed the many fraternal opportunities the Jewish groups offered. Another possible hypothesis is that the Jews of Nevada City and Grass Valley may have followed somewhat different Judaic rituals and practices. However, although it has been recorded that many Grass Valley Jews were observant, many Nevada City Jews, like the merchant Aaron Baruh, were also.

Nevada City boasted at least four separate Jewish organizations during the Gold Rush period. In Nevada City, the *Nevada Journal* of September 17, 1852, announced: "Notice. The Israelites of Nevada hereby present their sincere thanks to the officers and members of Nevada Lodge no. 13 of F. & A. Masons, for extending to them the free use of their hall for religious ceremonies. By Order of the Committee: A. Rosenheim, I. Grauman, L. Heilbronn." By 1854, the Nevada City Hebrew Society was founded and land bought for a cemetery

Gravestone of Melville Casper. Nevada City Jewish Cemetery. Photo: Ira Nowinksi/Judah L. Magnes Museum. Western Jewish History Center.

(and possibly an adjacent mortuary); the first known burial was that of Caroline Himes in 1856. The *Nevada Journal* noted in 1855 that this organization met at a Mr. Lachman's house [perhaps Benjamin. See below] and planned to procure a *Sefer Torah* (the first five books of Moses) and a *shofar* (the ram's horn used for *Rosh Hashanah* and *Yom Kippur*). Sarah Lodge No. 4 of the Ancient Order Kesher Shel Barzel, an organization similar to B'nai B'rith, was founded in Nevada City in 1873. In later years, the Jews of Nevada City and Grass Valley supported a single Jewish fraternal organization.

In 1868 the town's Eureka Social Club was founded, and described thus by "Sinbad" a correspondent for San Francisco's *Hebrew:* "There is probably not another town in California, aside from San Francisco and Sacramento, where the Hebrew element exercises a greater influence than they do in Nevada City. The Eureka Social Club, which has been organized nearly a year and is controlled by Israelites, has had much to do in increasing this influence, and socially speaking, has done much to harmonize society. The Club gave one masquerade ball last winter, and a subscription dance ball on Thanksgiving evening, both of which were highly successful and the latter particularly surpassed anything of the kind ever before witnessed in this city."

Newspaper advertisements document the variety and number of retail establishments owned by Jews. The following sampling gives some idea of the scope. In 1853 Simon Rosenthal & Brothers advertised black and colored silks and French and English merino wools, and in 1854, the store advertised its fireproof building. In contrast, Grauman & Josephson, who owned the Kentucky Store, advertised that they would sell at twenty-five percent cheaper than could be bought in brick buildings. Newbauer & Company sold eleven brands of cigars, as well as figs, oranges, raisins, nuts, and candy. Louis Dreyfuss ran a saloon and the United States Bakery at 22 Pine Street, and later founded the Milwaukee Brewery at the corner of Pine and Spring Streets. Aaron Baruh owned the Family Grocery Store, and in the 1860s ran a saloon; like many other Jews, Baruh, owned mining claims, often first received as payment for goods. Merchants David and Herman Shirpser left Nevada City for the Fraser River in Canada when gold was discovered there in 1858.

Jews were active participants in the Nevada City's affairs. Among the many examples: in 1857 Jacob Kohlman was a city trustee; Abraham Goldsmith was treasurer in 1871–72, and L.W. Dreyfuss was city treasurer before 1880 and served as a delegate to the Democratic county convention; S. Kohlman, Simon Mayers, Aaron Baruh, and J. Jacobs organized the Volunteer Rifle Company in 1858; and A. Rosenheim and J.M. Levy served on committees for a ball sponsored in 1856 by the Nevada Rifles. Rosenheim also acted in local theater.

## A Leading Family

The Baruh family were leading citizens of Nevada City for many decades. Their history gives a wonderful glimpse of how such "leading families" intertwined and often continue in prominence to this day. Aaron Baruh and his brother Herman arrived in 1852. They first went into the clothing business, but were burned out in the disastrous fires of 1856 and 1858. Aaron Baruh, it is subsequently recorded,

Gravestone of David Baruh. Nevada City Jewish Cemetery. Photo: Ira Nowinksi/ Judah L. Magnes Museum. Western Jewish History Center.

received gold dust and gold coins in his post-1858 grocery store.

Both Baruh brothers were active in the Jewish community and close to many other leaders. Herman Baruh was vice-president of the Nevada Hebrew Society in 1858, when Jacob Kohlman was president; Aaron Baruh bought the house at 816 Main Street, built by Kohlman in 1852. The *Nevada Journal* reported that the Nevada Hebrew Society celebrated its fifth anniversary with a fundraiser at Herman Baruh's house. Aaron Baruh was president of the Nevada Hebrew Benevolent Society in 1867 and a Third Degree member of the Grass Valley Garizim Lodge of B'nai B'rith in the 1870s and 1880s. Further, the Aaron Baruh family is said to have kept separate dishes for the Passover celebration and ordered *matzot* from San Francisco for the holiday.

Aaron Baruh married Rosalie Wolf on October 22, 1861 in Nevada City. The couple's *ketubah* (Jewish marriage contract) was signed by Jacob C. Marks and Simon Rosenthal; Solomon Rosenthal served as "officiating minister." (According to Jewish custom, a lay member of the congregation may perform a marriage.) The Baruhs' marriage certificate is still recorded in the Nevada County Clerk's and Recorder's Office. Aaron and Rosalie had seven children: Clara, Mose, Marcus, Joseph, David, Jennie, and Rebecca. The Jenny Ledge, a mining claim of Aaron Baruh, is named after daughter Jennie.

Jennie Baruh later married Isadore Zellerbach, son of Gold Rush pioneer banker Anthony Zellerbach of Moore's Flat. Anthony and his brother Marks Zellerbach engaged in mining activities in the Northern Mines, as well as in transportation and banking. Following financial reverses, Anthony moved to San Francisco where he turned a small paper and stationery establishment into the industry giant, Zellerbach Paper Company, later known as the Crown Zellerbach Corporation. Jennie Baruh Zellerbach never lost her connection with her Nevada City roots, acting as benefactor in the pioneer Jewish cemetery preservation effort. Today, Jennie and Isadore Zellerbach's grandson Stephen Zellerbach, chairs the Commission for the Preservation of Pioneer Jewish Cemeteries and Landmarks.

### The Lachman Family

The large number of children's graves in the Nevada City Jewish Cemetery is a stark reminder of the high rate of infant mortality, the devastation of epidemics, and the precarious nature of medical care in the 1850s and 1860s. In one striking example, all of eight graves in the Lachman family plot are the burial places of the children of Benjamin and Dora Lachman. Benjamin Lachman, a merchant in Nevada City and trustee of the Nevada Hebrew Society (later known as the Nevada Hebrew Benevolent Society), was in the hardware business in 1856, was a pawnbroker on Main Street in the 1860s, and later was in the clothing business. After young Joseph Lachman's death in 1866, the *Nevada Daily Transcript* reported: "The bereaved parents have buried two children within two weeks and a third one will be consigned to the grave today. They have lost all except one girl, and she is so ill that doubts are entertained of her recovery." We must wonder yet what devastation struck these children down.

### Jewish Historic Sites

◆ Baruh home, 516 Main Street, built by Jacob Kohlman in 1852 and purchased by Baruh in 1866. It is said that a *mezuzah* (a parchment scroll containing passages from Deut. 6:9 and 11:20 in a decorative case) is on every doorpost in the house. *Not open to the public.* The house is still owned by descendants of Aaron Baruh.

### Worth a Visit

◆ Nevada County Museum in Firehouse I, 214 Main Street

◆ Malakoff Diggins State Historical Park, north of Nevada City on Highway 49. This hydraulic mining site features exhibits and a museum.

# NEVADA CITY
# ⋙ THE CEMETERY ⋘

## Cemetery Facts

**Name:** Nevada City Jewish Cemetery
**Founded:** 1854
**First burial:** 1856
**Last burial:** 1890
**Rededicated as historic site:** October 29, 1972
**Number of gravestones visible:** 29.
Several loose stones appear to have been parts of gravestones, but additional grave sites have not been determined at this time.
**Site characteristics:** This cemetery is *difficult to find*. There is no sign marking the narrow, private road as the drive leading to the Jewish cemetery. After you have driven down the narrow access road, park in front of the gate to the chainlink fence at the cemetery entrance. Please be sure to leave a clear driveway for the occupant of the private house. Once inside the padlocked gate to the cemetery grounds, you will have to walk about seventy-five feet on uneven terrain to reach the chain-link fenced cemetery.

Buses will not be able to maneuver or turn around on the narrow drive.
**Special arrangements:** There is a padlocked gate. For information and access arrangements, please

call or write the Western Jewish History Center, Judah L. Magnes Museum, 2911 Russell Street, Berkeley, California 94705, (510) 549-6950. The Museum is open Sunday through Thursday from 10 to 4.

## Walking Tour

As you walk these paths, you will notice that for some of the individuals buried in these sacred grounds there is much more information in this guide than appears on their gravestone. For others the only information is a gravestone and carved inscription. Sadly, some stones have been too badly damaged to decipher a name; some stones are missing and for some only a foundation or a raised mound of earth remains.

For some individuals we have information from such sources as: recorded deeds and contracts,

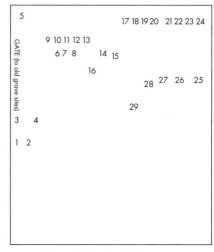

Nevada City Jewish Cemetery

newspaper articles and advertisements, minute books, diaries, letters, photographs, family histories and family trees, etc. And yet, there are those who shared in the Jewish experience in the California Gold Rush whose lives leave little or no permanent record.

*Upon entering the cemetery, turn to your right and proceed to the last gravestone along the fence to your right to begin your tour.*

1.  **Rebecca Heyman** (died February 16, 1874, age 48 years).

She was a native of Baden, Germany and the wife of Solomon Heyman. It is reported that the Heymans were "arrested for receiving and disposing property stolen from freight cars of the Central Pacific Railroad." A theory holds that Rebecca Heyman committed suicide after leaving the stage bound for Truckee. The theory is of particular interest since traditional Jewish practice does not allow the burial of suicides in consecrated soil.

2.  **Unknown grave.**

3.  **Melony Kohlman** (died December 27, 1878, age 24 years).

She was a native of New Orleans and the wife of Jacob Kohlman, who was an early leader in the Jewish community (see "Glimpses of the Pioneer Jewish Community.") From the 1850s, Jacob and Sol Kohlman operated a clothing store,

The Emporium of Fashion, on Main Street.

4.  **Unknown grave.**

There is a base only.

*To reach #5, proceed to the fence to the left of the gate.*

5.  **Melville Casper** (November 27, 1879–April 23, 1894, son of Kaskill Casper).

Thirteen-year-old Melville Casper died as a result of a boating accident in the Manzanita Mine Reservoir. His father, Kaskill Casper, was a successful business man in Nevada City, owner of The Clothier in the late 1870s and holder of many mining claims, including shares in the important Harmony Mine. The elder Casper was active in city government and was involved with the initial efforts to light Nevada City with incandescent lighting, although he was subsequently forced out of the lighting business there. He moved to Vallejo, California, and there he successfully continued investment in the business of new community lighting.

DREYFUSS FAMILY PLOT (6–13)

6.  **Louis W. Dreyfuss** (1890, age 65).

A native of Germany, he was an older cousin of Captain Alfred Dreyfus of France, whose false imprisonment would ultimately bring the issue of anti-Semitism to international focus. Louis Dreyfuss was an officer in Kesher Shel Barzel and a Third Degree member of Garizim Lodge of B'nai B'rith. (See also his many activities noted in "Glimpses of the Pioneer Jewish Community.") Dreyfuss owned considerable property in Nevada City. He and his wife had twelve children, four of whom are buried in the family plot.

"M.D. Thompson," carved at the bottom of the Louis Dreyfuss' column, appears to be the name of the stonecarver.

7. **Isadore Abraham Salaman** (died August 22, 1856, age 14 months).

He was the son of Abraham Salaman, a successful grocer in Grass Valley. Maria Salaman, Isadore's sister, is buried in the Grass Valley Jewish cemetery.

8. **Regina Dreyfuss** (died February 10, 1860, age 5 days, daughter of Louis W. Dreyfuss and wife).

   **Louisa Dreyfuss** (born May 31, 1865, died November 2, 1865, age 5 months, daughter of Louis W. Dreyfuss and wife).

This stone is broken.

The inscriptions for Regina and Louisa are on the same stone.

9. **Unknown grave.**

10. **Grace [?].**

This stone is illegible. The words "dau—of" are barely visible. No further information is known at this time.

11. **Ludwig Dreyfuss** (died August 19, 1880, son of Louis W. Dreyfuss and wife).

The *Union* stated that a fatal accident occurred when Ludwig climbed too near the brewery vat, lost his balance, and fell into boiling beer. This stone is badly broken and needs repair.

12. **Martin Dreyfuss** (died August 13, 1873, son of Louis W. Dreyfuss and wife).

Martin died of the croup.

13. **Raphael Rosenthal** (died January 24, 1868, age 4 years, son of S. and H. Rosenthal).

Solomon Rosenthal and his brother were in the dry goods business. There is a carved lamb on the stone.

The relationship of Raphael Rosenthal and Isadore Salaman to the Dreyfuss family is unknown at this time.

14. **Unknown grave.**

15. **Fannie Hyman** (died August 6, 1886, age 1 year and 3 months).

Several Hyman families were active merchants in Nevada City. A clothing establishment, the San Francisco Opposition Store, was owned by five Hyman brothers; also, there were wholesale grocers with the family name Hyman in Nevada City, with branches in San Francisco and New York.

16. **David Baruh** (died April 15, 1877, son of Aaron and Rosalie Wolf Baruh).

David died of pneumonia (For further information on the Baruh family, see this chapter's "Glimpses of the pioneer Jewish community.")

LACHMAN FAMILY PLOT (17–24)

17. **Jacob Lachman** (born May 1, 1859, died June 3,1859, son of Benjamin and Dora Lachman).

18. **Semi Lachman** (born March 20, 1860, died [?] 1860, [son or daughter] of Benjamin and Dora Lachman).

19. **Amanda Lachman** (born April 26, 1862).

This is a broken stone and only the date of birth is legible.

20. **[?] Lachman.**

There is a base only.

21. **[?] Lachman** (born August 21, 1864, died September 29, 1884).

Only the bottom half of the stone remains.

22. **Jennie Lachman** (died February 21, 1866).

This is a broken stone and only the date of death is legible.

23. **Joseph Lachman** (born August 25, 1863, died March 30, 1866).

24. **[Lachman].**

There is a base only. A piece of a gravestone contains a barely visible, although not readable, death date.

(See this chapter's "Glimpses of the Pioneer Jewish Community" for a description of the Lachman family.)

25. **Unknown grave.**

No name is left on this fragment of stone. The inscription reads "native of Winweiler, Rhenish, Bavaria, who departed this life May 20, 1857, in the 28th year of her age."

26. **Amelia Miller** (died of pneumonia on December 9, 1878, age 47 years).

She was the wife of Bernhart H. Miller who was in the clothing business.

27. **Caroline Himes** (died July 20, 1856, wife of L. Himes).

This is the oldest known grave in the Nevada City Hebrew Cemetery. It is possible that Caroline Himes was a victim of the July 19, 1856, fire that swept Nevada City.

28. **Unknown grave.**

There is a base only.

29. **Unknown grave.**

There is a base only.

# GRASS VALLEY
## ❦ THE COMMUNITY ❦

## Community Overview

Grass Valley, a mere four miles from Nevada City, gained its name from the rolling grasslands which define the local terrain. In the first years of the Gold Rush, cattle could be seen grazing in the valley, but already by 1851 this idyllic vision was obscured by a tent city of close to 20,000 miners. In 1850, it is said, George McKnight had stumbled upon quartz rock that glittered in the moonlight, revealing a vein of gold embedded deep in the stone. With this discovery, the methods and economics of gold mining in Grass Valley had dramatically changed. The lone miner with the pan swishing in the stream, or even the pair of miners using a sluice box, was soon replaced by large organizations holding significant investments in the massive and expensive mining equipment needed to burrow deep into the earth and to retrieve the gold from the rock. The owners themselves did not burrow into the earth, of course, but hired hundreds of employees, including many experienced miners from Cornwall in England, to run the equipment. The Empire

Mine, during its years of operation (1850 to 1956), yielded more than five million ounces of gold. Even the fiery dancer Lola Montez and her protégé, Lotta Crabtree, both of whom danced during the Gold Rush decades in Grass Valley could not eclipse the drama of hard rock mining for Grass Valley citizens.

## Glimpses of the Pioneer Jewish Community

As noted in the chapter on Nevada City, the adjacent communities of Grass Valley and Nevada City supported separate Jewish organizations. In 1856 the Shaar Zedek (Gates of Righteousness) Hebrew Benevolent Society of Grass Valley was formed for the express purpose of "taking charge of the cemetery, taking care of the sick, and burying the dead." In the February 13, 1857, edition of the San Francisco's

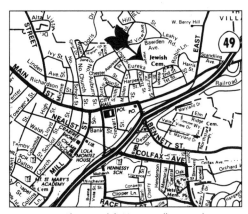

Directions to Shaar Zedek (Grass Valley Jewish cemetery): From Highway 49 take the Grass Valley Historic District exit (Colfax Highway 174), and turn right onto E. Main Street. Proceed on Main Street and turn left at Eureka Street. Proceed up the hill. Turn left on Second Street. The cemetery is on your right, bound by Blossom Lane, Second Street, and Eureka Street.

*Weekly Gleaner*, editor Rabbi Julius Eckman reported the words of Grass Valley resident Jacob C. Marks: "Allow me to inform you that our Society is in a flourishing condition. We were organized September 8th, 1856, and have since that time purchased a *Sepher Torah* [sic], with the necessary appendages, and also a Shophar [ram's horn for High Holiday services]. We have, too, a fine, well-fenced cemetery, with a substantial building on it, with all the implements required by our rites. May they never be wanted." A *Sefer Torah* from Grass Valley was donated to Congregation Emanu-El, San Francisco, after the 1906 earthquake and fire destroyed their Torah.

In later years, the Garizim Lodge No. 43 of B'nai B'rith, founded in 1861, replaced the Hebrew Benevolent Society in overseeing the cemetery and caring for community needs. The thriving Jewish world of Grass Valley, consisting of merchants, bankers, and investors in the mines survived well into the 1880s, probably as a result of Grass Valley's flourishing hard rock mining economy. In one outstanding example, the Weissbein brothers, Jacob and Joseph, who in the early years worked for their brother-in-law Jacob Hyman in his dry goods business at Mill and Bank Streets, established the Bank of Weissbein Brothers in 1876. According to local historian Michel Janicot, "The brothers acquired much property, land tracts, and several mining operations, includ-

ing the well-known Work Your Own Diggins and the Pittsburg Gold Flat Mine." The street adjacent to the Jewish cemetery was once known as Weissbein Avenue, and Joseph Weissbein once owned a property at Neal and South School Streets that had previously been owned by the Hebrew Benevolent Society and possibly slated for a synagogue site.

## Worth a Visit

♦ Empire Mine State Historic Park, 10791 E. Empire St., Grass Valley

♦ North Star Mining Museum and Pelton Wheel Exhibit, Allison Road at Mill Street, Grass Valley

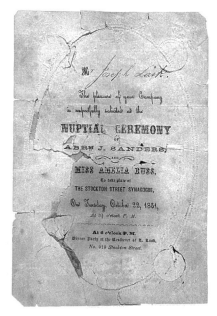

Wedding invitation of Abraham Sanders and Amelia Buss, married at Sherith Israel, San Francisco, 1861. The Sanders were residents of Grass Valley. Sherith Israel Congregation, San Francisco Collection. Western Jewish History Center.

# GRASS VALLEY
## ❧ THE CEMETERY ❧

## Cemetery Facts

**Name:** Shaar Zedek
**Founded:** 1856
**First burial:** 1857
**Last burial:** 1891
**Rededicated as historic site:**
September 13, 1970
**Number of gravestones visible:**
Approximately 30
Many of the stones in the cemetery
have crumbled, and grave sites are
often difficult to determine. The
stones in this cemetery seem particularly vulnerable to the destructive
elements of weather and time.
Many stones, which most likely
were originally vertical, now are
embedded horizontally in concrete
slabs.
**Site characteristics:** Less than one
acre remains of what was once a
five-acre plot of land purchased
by the Shaar Zedek Hebrew
Benevolent Society. A mortuary
building used to exist on the large
cemetery property; however, it is
not known where the structure was
located.
**Special arrangements:** There is a
padlocked gate. For information
and access arrangements, please
call or write the Western Jewish
History Center, Judah L. Magnes
Museum, 2911 Russell Street,
Berkeley, California 94705,

(510) 549-6950. The Museum is
open Sunday through Thursday
from 10 to 4.

## Walking Tour

As you walk these paths, you will
notice that for some of the individuals buried in these sacred grounds
there is much more information
in this guide than appears on their
gravestone. For others the only
information is a gravestone and
carved inscription. Sadly, some
stones have been too badly damaged to decipher a name; some
stones are missing and for some
only a foundation or a raised
mound of earth remains.

For some individuals we have
information from such sources
as: recorded deeds and contracts,
newspaper articles and advertisements, minute books, diaries, letters, photographs, family histories
and family trees, etc. And yet, there
are those who shared in the Jewish
experience in the California Gold

Shaar Zedek Cemetery, Grass Valley

Rush whose lives leave little or no permanent record.

*After unlocking the gate and entering the cemetery, turn to your left to begin the tour.*

1. **Clarence Morris Nathan** (died December 28, 1874, age 2 months, son of Nathan and Annie Nathan).

Nathan Nathan was an investor in the mines and in partnership with Morris Nathan, a clothing merchant. Nathan and Annie owned a house on South Auburn Street.

2. **Simon Harris** (died 1863, age 18 years).

A native of England, Simon may have been the son of B. Harris, an investor in mines who was also a tobacco and liquor merchant on Mill Street. Records also show that B. Harris and his wife Hannah sold an improved lot, with a brick building, to Abraham Salaman for three thousand dollars. This is a broken stone.

3. **Cecilia Nathan** (January 15, 1862, age 22 years).

In the *Nevada Daily Gazette*, January 16, 1867, is an account of Cecelia's death indicating that the young woman slipped and fell into a well "while in the act of drawing water." The article further speculated that the death may have been a suicide. Traditional Jewish custom does not allow a suicide to be buried in sacred ground.

4. **Issac Hirsch** (May 28, 1874, son of Samuel and Minna Hirsch).

In 1874, Samuel Hirsch had a tailor shop on Main Street.

5. **Celia Nathan** (1861, age 2 years, daughter of Benjamin J. Nathan).

Nevada County deed books show Benjamin Nathan's name on over fifty deeds between 1856 and 1860. And it is known that a B. Nathan was in the clothing business in Rough and Ready in 1856, and by 1861 was a partner of Jacob Morris in Grass Valley. Benjamin Nathan's estate was valued at over forty thousand dollars.

6. **Moses Goodman** (died May 1, 1862, son of E. and S. Goodman).

7. **Solomon Goodman** (born April 27, 1858–died April 22, 1862, son of E. and S. Goodman).

The father is possibly the E. Goodman, a merchant in the nearby town of Rough and Ready.

8. **Unknown grave.**

There is a base only.

9. **Unknown grave.**

There are a base and the bottom six inches of the stone with no legible writing.

10. **Abraham Levy** (died May 5, 1874, age 23).

He was the youngest son of Esther Levy of "Victoria, V.I. B.C."

Shaar Zedek Cemetery, Grass Valley. Gravestone of Louis Levy. Photo: Ira Nowinksi/ Judah L. Magnes Museum. Western Jewish History Center.

### 11. Louis Levy (1837–1871).

He was a native of Fordom, Prussia. "Erected by his nieces and nephews."

### 12. Elie Halphen (1800–1882).

Halphen was a native of Metz, France. An article in the *Nevada Daily Transcript* reported that Halphen had served as Captain in the French army and as mayor of Metz before leaving France, possibly as a result of family and political problems. In 1852, Halphen emigrated to Oakland, California where he owned considerable property. In the Gold Country, he invested in several mines, opened stores in Brown's Valley,

Yuba County, and in Grass Valley and was listed as a saloon keeper and grocer. It is said that Halphen's family, who remained in France, were successful capitalists.

### 13. Solomon Rosenthal (died 1878, age 62 years).

Rosenthal was a native of Margolin, Prussia. A Grass Valley merchant, he officiated at the High Holiday services in Nevada City in 1861 and at the wedding of Isadore Jacobs and Miss Singer in Nevada City in 1868. Solomon Rosenthal is possibly the father of Raphael Rosenthal, who died at age four in 1868 and is buried in Nevada City. This stone has a Hebrew inscription on the back which tells us that Solomon (Sholomo) was the son of Raphael and he died on Thursday the sixteenth of Kislev (December).

### 14. Cohn.

This stone is barely readable. According to Michel Janicot, it may be that Cohn is an infant who died on July 17, 1861.

### 15. Maria B. Salaman (died at five months, daughter of Abraham Salaman).

Maria's brother, Isadore Abraham, who died in 1856 at fourteen months of age, is buried in the Nevada City Cemetery. Abraham Salaman, the father of these two children, was a very successful grocer, liquor, mining supplies, and crockery retailer, and investor in real estate and mining properties.

Records show that, in 1856, Salaman was a partner in the Grass Valley firm of Silvester & Company, whose building had withstood the disastrous 1855 fire. City council minutes show that Salaman once protested the "house of ill-fame next to his dwelling." In 1866 Salaman and Martin Ford sold their interests in the Union Jack Mining Company to Lewis Gerstle for fifty thousand dollars. Gerstle figures prominently in Jewish Gold Rush history. In the early 1850s Lewis Gerstle and his partner, "forty-niner" Louis Sloss, ran a grocery store in Sacramento. Later, the successful entrepreneurial partners opened up the Alaskan fur trade with their San Francisco based Alaska Commercial Company.

**16. Unknown grave.**

There is a broken base only

**17. Benjamin Nathan** ( [?]slaw, Prussia, born or died 1873, son of [?] and Tzvi Nathan).

This stone is broken and indecipherable.

**18. Unknown grave.**

There is a base only.

**19. Judith Sanders** (died January 12, 1866, age 7 months and 13 days, daughter of Abraham I. and Amilie Sanders).

**20. Unknown grave.**

There is a base only.

**21. Unknown grave.**

There is a base only.

NOVITZKY FAMILY PLOT (22–23)

**22. Simon Novitzky** (1817–1891, a native of Prussia, husband of Sarah).

**Sarah Novitzky** (1822–1889, a native of Germany, wife of Simon).

Simon Novitzky was the owner of the Pioneer Hat Store on the corner of Mill and Bank Streets. Simon's brother, Henry, was a tailor in Nevada City in 1856, and by 1861 moved to Grass Valley where he was a retailer, and with Simon, invested in mining claims.

Sarah and Simon's names are inscribed on either side of this free standing column, one of the few markers still vertical in the Grass

Grave-stone of Simon and Sarah Novitzky. Shaar Zedek Cemetery, Grass Valley. Photo: Ira Nowinksi/Judah L. Magnes Museum. Western Jewish History Center.

Valley cemetery. The column is inscribed "We are not separated. We will meet again."

**23. S.N.** (most likely refers to Sarah Novitzky).

**24. Unknown grave.**

**25. Simon Abraham** (died December 17, 1865, age 44 years).

He was a native of Nakel, Prussia, and the brother of Hyman Abraham buried in plot 28.

**26. Unknown grave.**

One can barely make out "Louis" on this broken stone.

**27. Henry J. Steler** (1869–1875, son of Pepi and E. Steler).

It is reported that Henry died of scarlet fever. Pepi may have been the P. Steler who was a jeweler and watchmaker on Main Street. There is a faded flower engraved on this column. "Pepi" is often the nick-name of Joseph.

**28. Hyman Abraham** (died July 16, 5617 [1857], 32 years).

He was a native of Nachel Province, Posen. Hyman Abraham is the first known burial in Shaar Zedek Cemetery. He was the brother of Simon Abraham [buried in plot 25] and owned property on Main Street, Grass Valley valued at fifteen hundred dollars. The bottom of this stone is engraved "R. Myers & Co. 747 Market St. S.F."

**29. Unknown grave.**

There is a broken stone which is indecipherable.

**30. Unknown grave.**

There is a base only.

Shaar Zedek Cemetery, Grass Valley. Gravestone of Henry Steler. Photo: Ira Nowinksi/Judah L. Magnes Museum. Western Jewish History Center.

# MARYSVILLE
## ❧ THE COMMUNITY ❧

### Marysville Overview

Marysville, located at the confluence of the Yuba and Feather Rivers, gained prominence in the Gold Rush years as a key supply station for the Northern Mines. Particularly before the advent of the railroads, Marysville boasted a thriving river trade, with its merchants supplying the clothing, tools, food, and household supplies for the mining communities in the interior. According to Robert Levinson, often the adventurous gold seeker, recently arrived in San Francisco from a long ocean voyage, would change to a smaller river steamboat and, by traveling up the Sacramento River arrive in Marysville within twenty-four hours, stopping only briefly for supplies before racing to the gold fields.

According to the chronicler I.J. Benjamin II in his work *Three Years in America,* Marysville could boast by 1856 of an active city council, of merchant and passenger steamboats tied up at the levee, of the United States Hotel on D Street, and of public gambling establishments, including one on First Street between D Street and Maiden Lane. There were also five Masonic Lodges, three Odd Fellows lodges, a Temple of Honor lodge which

acted as a benevolent society and worked for temperance, and a two-thousand-volume library. Marysville had built a courthouse in 1854 and by 1856 had several educational institutions, including the College of Notre Dame de Namur, an elementary school for male and female students, and a secondary school for women only. In 1863, Abraham Lincoln appointed Marysville resident Judge Stephan J. Field to the United States Supreme Court, the first "westerner" so appointed.

As in many Gold Rush towns, residents spoke a variety of languages and came from many cultures. Marysville had a significant Chinese population, and the com-

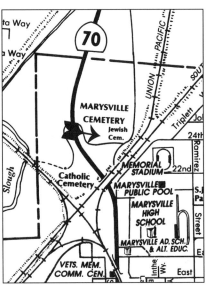

Marysville Hebrew Cemetery (Highway 70, just north of town): From Highway 20 west (from Grass Valley), turn right onto Highway 70. Continue past the brick Marysville High School. The cemetery is on the right side of the road, just past the overpass.

munity maintained its presence even during the years of the building of the railroads, when many Chinese were uprooted from their communities.

Marysville was named after the wife of Charles Covillaud, an early land owner. Mary Covillaud was a survivor of the Donner Party, the ill-fated wagon train stranded in the unforgiving snows of the Sierra Nevada.

## Glimpses of the Pioneer Jewish Community

The Marysville Jewish community followed an organizational pattern common to the Gold Rush communities. Its Hebrew Benevolent Society was organized in 1853, and as stated in its constitution "The funds of the society shall be appropriated as follows: relief to the poor, needy, sick, and the burial of the dead of the Jewish persuasion in Marysville and vicinity." In 1855 the officers of the Society were E. Newberger, president; J.S. Winehill, vice president; T. Hyman, treasurer; M. Marcuse, secretary; E. Katzenstein, K.L. Stone, M. Mendelson, J.S. Barman, and Jacob Meyers, directors.

The Marysville *Daily Evening Herald* of October 3, 1853, reported that a synagogue had been dedicated the day before. The article placed the synagogue in "the new brick building on C St., between 1st and 2nd, east side, up stairs."

In 1855, according to a deed recorded and dated that August 28,

the Marysville Hebrew Benevolent Society purchased land for a cemetery from the estate of Robert Buchanan, with the site described "commencing at the south east corner of the present City Cemetery." Records also indicate that the cemetery encompassed one square block, surrounded by a high brick wall, with a brick house on the property devoted to burial purposes.

Like other Gold Rush Jewish communities, the Marysville Jewish community was not isolated. For example, the 1851–1856 Minute Book of Congregation Sherith Israel, San Francisco, records a July 1852 solicitation of funds from the Jews of Marysville, Stockton, and Sonora for the construction of the newly formed synagogue; the chronicler I.J. Benjamin documented a visit to Marysville in the late 1850s; and the San Francisco *Hebrew* reported that on a visit to Marysville, Rabbi Notkin of Jerusalem, accredited by Sir Moses Montefiore, successfully raised funds for the Holy Land.

For a short time, Marysville supported two active Jewish fraternal organizations. In 1864 Lodge No. 56 (Mariam Lodge) of the Independent Order B'nai B'rith was organized. Its first officers were: S.R. Rosenthal, president; A. Suss, vice-president; R. Katz, secretary; S. Hochstadter, financial secretary; M. Slavyer, treasurer; M. Marcuse, monitor; and G. Cohn, warden. Between 1874 and 1877, Marysville had a local chapter of the Ancient

Simon Glazier, former Marysville merchant and his wife Clara Glazier, San Francisco circa 1880. Photo Archive Collection, Western Jewish History Center.

Jewish Order Kesher Shel Barzel. The local chapter included Fidelity Lodge No. 14 and Rebecca Lodge No. 6, the women's affiliate of the Fidelity. By the 1870s, however, many Jews had left the mining communities, including Marysville, and it seems that the Jewish popu- lation did not warrant two active groups.

On April 25, 1865, the *Marys- ville Daily Appeal* responded to President Lincoln's assassination:

> At a special meeting of the Marysville Hebrew Benevolent Society, held on Sunday, April 23, 1865, the following preamble and resolutions were unanimously adopted: Whereas, the mournful and sad news of the death of Abraham Lincoln, late President of the United States of America, has been announced to us;...and Whereas, the former has thrown our whole land in deep sorrow and affliction, while the latter has justly aroused the nation's wrath and execration, and deeming it our duty as citizens of one com- mon country to express our deep felt emotions upon this sad event.

Newspaper advertisements also show an active Jewish merchant community in Marysville from the early years of the Gold Rush through the first two decades of the twentieth century. Isaac and Simon Glazier operated the Old Corner Cigar Store from 1851 until 1862 when they moved to San Francisco. J.H. Marcuse advertised Optimo, clear Havana, and five-cent cigars for his Western and Palace Cigar Store. P. Brown advertised himself as "Marysville's leading tailor, pants made to order from $4.00 up and P. Brown's speciality, White Labor Overall." Schneider's Clothing, established in 1862 and existing well into the twentieth cen- tury, advertised itself as "the Home of Values."

## Worth a Visit

◆ Chinese Bok Kai Temple
  D Street at the Yuba River levee

## Cemetery Facts

**Name:** Marysville Hebrew Cemetery
**Founded:** 1855
**First burial:** 1855
**Last burial:** 1945
**Number of gravestones visible:**
Approximately 46. Many stones
are displaced and broken, making
gravesites difficult both to identify
and to count.
**Site characteristics:** The Jewish
cemetery is reached by entering the
Marysville City Cemetery gates and
turning right. An early description
mentions that the Jewish cemetery
is: "one block square, and is surrounded by a high brick wall that
cost one thousand dollars. The
society has also a brick house that
is used in connection with the
cemetery."

Many of the stones in the
Marysville cemetery show the
effects of weather, age, and neglect.
Some stones are lying in pieces on
the ground, often displaced from
their original position; others have
shifted off their bases and are
sheared in half. It is possible that
through the last 140 years, flooding
and subsequent silting of the landscape may have wreaked havoc with
the inscriptions as well as shifted the
position of the stones. In late 1994
the Commission for the Preservation

of Pioneer Jewish Cemeteries and
Landmarks filed a petition in the
Yuba County Court to be named
the successor organization to the
now defunct Marysville Hebrew
Benevolent Society and to assume
the Trusteeship of the Jewish cemetery. This petition was approved by
the court in July of 1995 and subsequently the Commission began the
painstaking and meticulous work of
restoration.
**Special arrangements:** If City
Cemetery gates are locked, you
may need to check with the
Marysville City Hall to arrange
for access.

## Walking Tour

As you walk these paths, you will
notice that for some of the individuals buried in these sacred grounds
there is much more information in
this guide than appears on their
gravestone. For others the only
information is a gravestone and
carved inscription. Sadly, some
stones have been too badly damaged to decipher a name; some

```
        46   45

    44 43   42   41 40 39 38 37
                 28 27
 36 35 34 33 32 31  30 29 26   25   24 23 22    21

   20 19 18 17 16      15        14        13

                    12    11   10  9  8

                          7 6    5 4 3 2 1
```

Marysville Hebrew Cemetery

stones are missing and for some only a foundation or a raised mound of earth remains.

For some individuals we have information from such sources as: recorded deeds and contracts, newspaper articles and advertisements, minute books, diaries, letters, photographs, family histories and family trees, etc. And yet, there are those who shared in the Jewish experience in the California Gold Rush whose lives leave little or no permanent record.

*After entering Marysville City Cemetery gate turn to your right and walk along the right fence, heading toward the east. The Jewish cemetery is on the southeast corner of the larger cemetery.*

1. **Hannah Davis** (died 1857, wife of Abraham Davis).

She was a native of Filehne, Prussia. A further inscription on the base of the stone refers to "also of her infant HANNAH by whom she was followed."

2. **Dona Levey** (born 1789, died 1859, native of Elbesee, Baden Germany).

3. **Simon Glucksman** (died August 26, 1859, age 24 years).

He was a native of Kempen, Prussia. The dramatic inscription on the stone includes considerable Hebrew writing below a carving of a broken tree limb. The English inscription states that Glucksman was "murdered on Friday, August 26, 1859 on the highway between

Gravestone of Julius Pier. Marysville Hebrew Cemetery. Photo: Bram Goodwin. Courtesy of Bram Goodwin.

La Porte and St. Louis." These latter cities were mining towns a few miles north of Marysville.

4. **Isaac Bensh** (died 1855, age 56 years, native of Prussia).

This appears to be the first burial in the Marysville Hebrew Cemetery.

5. **John Smith** (died 1866, age 46).

He was a native of Germany. A weeping tree is carved on the stone.

6. **Unknown grave.**

This appears to be a base and possible footstone.

7. **Julius Pier** (a.k.a. Joseph Pierre) (died 1895, age 63 years).

A native of Germany, Julius Pier, a merchant, was murdered in his store. The motive was reported as robbery.

*Begin row two*

8. **Samuel Rosenberg** (died January 3, 1877, age five months).

   **Simon Rosenberg** (died July 3, 1875).

   Samuel Rosenberg (died July 3, 1875, age 11 months, 24 days).

All inscriptions for the Rosenberg children are on a double stone, placed at the base. Only Simon's name is clearly visible.

Records do not identify the parents of the Rosenberg children, or indicate whether Samuel and Simon, who died on the same day in 1875, were brothers (twins?), or cousins. The close proximity of the graves probably indicates that this is a family plot, and that the second Samuel Rosenberg was named for the first.

The above three Rosenberg infant graves are broken and almost impossible to read. Extensive research in Marysville and Yuba County records by Commission member, Abraham Friedman, produced the above clarification, along with information about many other persons buried in the Marysville Hebrew Cemetery. Friedman also noted that numerous recorded listings did not yield observable stones in the cemetery. Dick Marquette, Marysville postman and local historian, also provided significant information on this cemetery and on the Jewish community, but much remains to be learned.

9. **Unknown grave.**

10. **Kuhn** (age 3 years).

    Base of stone only.

POPPER FAMILY PLOT (11)

11. **Samuel Popper** (died 1924, age 68 years, husband of Sarah).

A native of Austria, Popper ran a second hand store in Marysville at 309 Second Street with his partner, Adolph Krubas.

   **Sarah Popper** (died in 1918, age 58 years).

She was the wife of Samuel, and also a native of Austria.

   Samuel and Sarah are on the same stone.

12. **Eddy Armer** (died June 19, 1861, age 2 years, son of Max and Dorothea).

There is a Hebrew inscription on the reverse side of this stone. A merchant and a native of Germany, Max Armer, was a member of B'nai B'rith and in 1854, a member of the Yuba Engine Company. He died in San Francisco in 1904.

*Begin row three*

13. **Unknown grave.**

There is only a broken base.

14. **Unknown grave.**

There is only a broken base.

15. **Max Myers** (1859–1860, age 1 year, son of I. and H. Myers).

The inscription is partly illegible.

16. **Simon Weil** (son of H. and J. Weil).

There is a Hebrew inscription on the stone and a carving of a drooping tree. Hana Weil buried in plot #41 is most likely Simon's sister.

17. **Matilda [or Marilda] Weil** (died June 19, 1865, age 7 months, daughter of A. and L. Weil).

18. **Abe Cohn** (died May 13, 1866, son of A. and P. Cohn).

19. **Isaac Cohn** (son of A. and P. Cohn).

This stone is on the ground and the inscription is quite faded.

20. **[?] Raphael** (son of M. and P. Raphael).

This stone is broken.

*Begin row four*
*At the base of a large eucalyptus tree there appears to be the remains of an old brick wall; perhaps this was part of the mortuary building.*

21. **Unknown grave or graves.**

This seems to be the remains of a family plot at the base of a large tree.

KATZENSTEIN FAMILY PLOT (22–24)

There is an obelisk on the ground, noting the following four burials. "Children of M. Katzenstein" is inscribed on the obelisk.

22. **Gabriel Katzenstein** (died May 11, 1878, age 59 years, native of France).

This inscription is on the base of an obelisk, which is on the ground. There is a footstone inscribed "G.K."

**Arthur Katzenstein** (died Nov. 1853).

**Armon Katzenstein** (died Dec. 25, 1862).

**Rene Katzenstein** (died Jan. 26, 1871).

23. **Arthur Katzenstein** (born June 6, 1853, died November 1853, age 5 months, son of E. and M. Katzenstein).

24. **Armon Katzenstein** (1859–1862, child of E. and M. Katzenstein).

An apparent footstone is broken.

25. **Unknown grave or graves.**

There appears to be a stone border for a family plot. No fragments of gravestones are in the immediate vicinity.

26. **Julius Worms** (died July 3, 1885, age 83 years).

He was a native of France.

BROWN FAMILY PLOT (27–28)

27. **Royal Brown** (died April 21, 1871, age 11 years).

At the bottom right of the stone is the inscription "Shafer and Company," the same inscription found on the Strouse stone in Mokelumne Hill.

**28. Franklin Lowery Brown** (died April 10, 1871, age 4 years).

In the 1990s Royal and Franklin Brown's headstones were found near the cemetery gate, fifty to sixty yards from the other Brown gravestones. The two stones have been placed near the Brown family plot, awaiting further research.

**29. Bertha Cohn** (1841–1871, wife of Simon Cohn).

A native of Fordon, Prussia, she died in Quincy, California.

**30. Harry Barnett** (died February 7, 1873, age 55 years).

He was a native of England. An advertisement from 1860 states "H. Barnett's Grand Gift Enterprise will take place at the Marysville Theater on the 12th Day of June 1860. Grand Dramatic Entertainment. $5,000.00 in prizes. Tickets $1.00...One Bar of Gold— Actual Value $500.00...one of the most splendid assortments of Gifts ever presented at any Entertainment in the State, and to be conducted with the same liberal fairness which characterized his two former efforts."

**31. Nathan Cohn** (1853–1872).

**32. Isedore Silverstein** (1837–1871).

He was a native of Schneidmuehl, Prussia. The word "Seward" is possibly visible on the bottom of the stone. Perhaps Seward was the stonecarver. The base of this stone is on the ground and separated from the base.

**33. Unknown grave.**

There is a base only.

**34. Hanchen Meyer Hirschfelder** (1830–1869, wife of Emanuel H. Hirschfelder).

She was a native of Carlsruhe, Baden, Germany. A letter from Hanchen to her family in Germany is at the Western Jewish History Center. It describes her journey to the gold fields.

**35. Bertha [?].**

This broken gravestone may possibly be that of Bertha Hirschfelder who died at age six months and was the daughter of V. and T. Hirschfelder. A brick lining to the grave is partially visible.

**36. Bertha Weiss** (died December 6, 1890, age 3 years, daughter of Abraham and Malvina Birnbaum Weiss).

Malvina arrived from Germany in 1883 to stay with her uncle Nathan Schneider, an early member of the Marysville Jewish Community, who served as an officer in Kesher Shel Barsel. Nathan owned Schneider Clothing on 2nd and D Streets, and after his death, his niece Malvina and her husband Abraham ran the store until 1920. When Nathan's wife Rosa died, Malvina and Abraham took care of the Schneider children. The family home, located at 635 D Street, was built in 1850 by the prominent Marysville pioneer, Judge Field. According to Fred Weiss, a great-nephew of Malvina Weiss, the family home stood on a 25 foot lot, was built of bricks brought around Cape Horn, and had early gas lighting and wallpaper of pressed metal. Weiss remembers that when he visited in the 1930s, the three-story house still had no indoor toilet facilities.

*Begin row five*

ABRAHAM FAMILY PLOT (37)

**37. Abraham Abrahams** (1856–1920, husband of Tina Abrahams).

He was a clothing merchant.

**Tina Abrahams** (1868–1913, died at age 44 years).

She was a native of Marysville, wife of Abraham Abrahams, daughter of Philip Brown, and mother of Jacob and Harry Abrahams.

The stone with Abraham's inscription is broken off the

Gravestone of A. Abraham. Marysville Hebrew Cemetery. Photo: Bram Goodwin. Courtesy of Bram Goodwin.

pedestal. In addition there are two small markers. One bears the inscription "A.A." and the other "T.A."

**38. Fannie Brown** (died September 39, 1890, age 35 years, wife of Philip Brown).

**39. Philip Brown** (died May 30, 1899, age 63 years, husband of Fannie and Hanchen).

A native of Russia, he ran the P. Brown & Brothers Clothing Store, located in the town's Odd Fellows Building. He advertised as a merchant and tailor shop with goods from the "East, Oregon, California, and France."

**40. Hanchen Brown** (died September 29, 1877, age 35 years, wife of Philip Brown).

This stone is carved with a draped motif.

**41. Hana Weil** (died July 7, 1871).

Simon Weil buried in plot #16 is most likely Hana's brother.

**42. Unknown grave.**

There is a base only.

**43. Louis Goldman** (died 1869, age 3 [or 36?] years).

He was a native of Mistefeld, Bavaria.

**44. Jeanette Marcuse** (died December 12, 1874, age 70).

She was the wife of Abraham Marcuse, a native of Filene, Germany. Jeanette died as the

result of an accident. Abraham
Marcuse, a native of Berlin, first
arrived in the United States in 1847
and ran a candy store in Philadelphia,
where the famed Wanamaker's
Department Store was later located. Among Abraham and Jeanette's
sons were Marcus, Meyer, and
Jonas. There is an M. Marcuse listed as the Treasurer of the Hebrew
Benevolent Soceity in 1855, and as
Monitor of the B'nai B'rith in 1864.
Jonas Marcuse engaged in a variety
of businesses in Marysville, including ranch land along the Feather
River; however, heavy flooding
caused by the placer mining up-
stream caused the business to fail.
Jonah Marcuse, a grandson of
Abraham and Jeanette's, was elected treasurer of Sutter County, a
county adjacent to Marysville. In
1911 plans which were never
implemented were filed for the
subdivision of Marcuse Colony,
Subdivision No. 1, Sutter County.

Gravestone of Jeanette Marcuse. Marysville
Hebrew Cemetery. Photo: Bram Goodwin.
Courtesy of Bram Goodwin.

*Begin row six*

SCHWAB AND WEIST FAMILY PLOT
(45–46)

45. **Ray Weist** (1882–1923).

46. **Moses Schwab** (1855–1925,
    husband of Pauline Schwab).

    **Pauline Schwab** (1857–1945,
    wife of Moses Schwab, daugh-
    ter of Ray Weist).

# COLUMBIA STATE
## ❋ HISTORIC PARK ❋

## *Tour Note*

You will find that Columbia State Historic Park is an important stop on your tour of the pioneer Jewish cemeteries, even though the town does not have a Jewish cemetery. The accurately restored and recreated town of Columbia provides a rare opportunity to step back in time and experience community life during the Gold Rush years.

In 1945, the State of California purchased the land and dilapidated buildings in the commercial area of Columbia and began the restoration process. Buildings were restored or rebuilt using historic records, many of which are housed in the fascinating William Cavalier Museum archives. Research and restoration projects are ongoing.

In Columbia, take a few hours to relax. Pan for gold; take a stagecoach ride; visit the apothecary, the Chinese Joss House, and the Columbia Fire House. Walk the path to the 1860 Columbia Grammar School; stop by the Wells Fargo Office; have a sarsaparilla at the saloon; and be sure to explore the museum. There is ample evidence of a thriving Jewish community in Columbia during the Gold Rush years.

## *The Community*
### *Columbia Overview*

In March of 1850, a mining party, led by Thaddeus and George Hildreth, was stuck in a rainstorm and, while waiting for their blankets to dry, discovered gold near their make-shift camp. The first name of the town was Hildreth's Diggins. The first town officer, Major Richard Sullivan, held the title of *alcalde* (Spanish for mayor), reflective of the early Mexican influence in the gold camps. Under Alcade Sullivan, the camp changed its name to Columbia, Gem of the Southern Mines.

By April of 1850, the population in what was then called the

Stagecoach. From *The Autobiography of Charles Peters.*

American Camp (to distinguish it from the nearby Mexican claim) was close to eight thousand persons. In those early years, gamblers were part of the often transient, strike-it-rich population, and an early *Miners and Business Men's Directory* states: "At one time there was [sic] one hundred and forty-three monte-banks in operation, the funds of which amounted to not less than half a million of dollars. It was common to see men turn a card for three and four thousand dollars."

Water rights have historically played an important role in California economics and politics, and Columbia had its share of battles over these rights, vital to placer mining. In 1851 the Tuolumne County Water Company was organized to build a ditch to ensure running water for placer mining. A Sacramento banker, D.O. Mills, contributed three hundred thousand dollars for the water project, which extended all the way to the South Fork of the Stanislaus River. By 1855 high water rates prompted a strike by the placer miners and the creation of the rival Columbia and Stanislaus River Water Company, which built a major flume system. Water was not only vital to the mining industry but was also necessary to control the many fires that often engulfed the wood buildings of the Mother Lode towns.

## Glimpses of the Pioneer Jewish Community

Some histories of Columbia indicate that the first Odd Fellows Hall, destroyed in the devastating fire of 1857, was used as a synagogue during High Holidays. In later years, High Holidays were celebrated upstairs in the Masonic Lodge on Washington Street. By 1859, the Jewish community of Columbia had joined with the Sonora Hebrew Benevolent Society to carry out Jewish traditions and to bury the dead. However, the Jews of Columbia participated in their town's own economic, political, and social life.

Phillip Schwartz was the owner of the New York Dry Goods Store, located on Main Street between State and Fulton, next door to the Sam Leon building and up the street both from J. Levy and Sons Dry Goods Store and from Levy Brothers Dry Goods Store. In an ad in the *Columbia Weekly Times* of August 8, 1861, Schwartz described some of his merchandise as follows "For bonnets, mantillas, caps, collars and shawls; dresses for breakfasts, and dinners, and balls; silk, muslin, and lace, crape [sic], velvet and satin, brocade and broadcloth, and other material quite as expensive and much more ethereal."

There were at least two merchant Levy families active in the Columbia community. Joel Levy, a native of Posen, Poland, owned the J. Levy and Sons Dry Good Store with his sons Abraham, Harris, David, and Louis. The other Levy merchant family owned Levy Brothers Dry Goods, later called S. and H. Levy and then The Three Brothers.

Harris Morris Levy, the owner of the latter establishment, arrived in California by 1854 with his wife Sarah Abrahams Levy; Harris and Sarah were natives of Naklo, Poland. A family story recounts that the ship the Levys were taking to California was wrecked off the Cuban coast, and the couple remained for a few years in Cuba before continuing to California, bound for Columbia—perhaps to meet up with the established businessman Isaac Levy.

Another pioneer, Bernhard Marks came to California in 1851 from New England to seek his fortune. His letters to his cousin, Dr. Jacob Solis-Cohen of Philadelphia, provide valuable documentation on life in San Francisco and in the small mining towns during the early years. Marks mined claims in Placerville, and later, Jamestown before settling in Columbia in 1860. In Columbia, he and his wife, Cornelia Barlow Marks, ran a successful private school, yet in 1861, Bernhard Marks faced overt anti-Semitic opposition when he sought the position of public school teacher, and school board candidates ran for the specific purpose of defeating his appointment. The *Columbia Tuolumne Courier* of April 11, 1861, contained the

following letter:

> What created the wicked, illiberal, and unmanly excitement at the late school elections: Simply the fact that the only man in the city who, in common honesty could have been appointed teacher of the public school, is not a member of their (newly elected trustees) church, and does not participate in their version of Divine services.

It is probable that Cornelia Barlow Marks is not related to the Barlows buried in the Sonora Hebrew Cemetery. An article in *Western States Jewish Historical Quarterly* states that Cornelia Barlow's family had been in New York and Connecticut since the Revolutionary War and were not Jewish.

# ❊ THREE-DAY TOUR ❊ OF THE PIONEER JEWISH CEMETERIES

Whether or not you have time to visit all seven cemeteries described in this book during your visit to the Gold Country, a glance at the following tour will give you an indication of the distance involved and the overall Gold Country experience.

The tour starts in Sonora, the most southern of the pioneer Jewish cemeteries, and proceeds north along Highway 49 to Grass Valley and Nevada City. It then heads southwest on Highway 20 towards Marysville in the Sacramento Delta; subsequently it turns south via Highways 70 and 5 to the final destination of Old Town, Sacramento. Naturally, you may reverse the suggested itinerary, or you may wish to focus on only one or two cemeteries, and their respective towns.

In addition to the cemetery visits, ample time is available for exploration, meals, and travel. The tour is designed to allow time for your individual interests. The daily itinerary does not include specific recommendations for meals or lodging, but does suggest possible timing for these stops.

A few additional optional sites of interest are suggested. Note, however, that if all suggested sites are visited, several additional hours may need to be added to each tour day, or a fourth day added to your trip. You will want to consider your own interests and the time you have available, in determining the season for travel as well as your trip's focus. Remember that the best touring leaves plenty of free time for sampling local events such as fairs, festivals, flea markets, theaters, and the like.

If you can only take one day, it is possible, if ambitious, to cover the Sonora to Jackson segment of the tour. Likewise, one can cover the Placerville to Grass Valley segment (without Marysville and Sacramento) in a full day. As the cemeteries have no artificial lighting, please consider the number of daylight hours available in planning your visits.

The California Gold Country is a popular vacation destination during the summer months, late spring, and early fall. It is recommended that you obtain one of the many fine guidebooks available regarding lodging, restaurants, historic sights, and recreation opportunities in the region.

Be sure to check the visiting hours of the museums and other historic sites. It is important to call the Western Jewish History Center of the Judah L. Magnes Museum, (510) 549-6950, Monday through

Thursday, 10–4, for information regarding specific entry arrangements for the Sonora, Placerville, Nevada City, and Grass Valley pioneer Jewish cemeteries. Other entry arrangements may need to be made for the Marysville and Sacramento pioneer Jewish cemeteries.

# Tour of the Pioneer Jewish Cemeteries of the Gold Country

DAY ONE: SONORA TO JACKSON

### Sonora, "The Queen of the Southern Mines"

◆ Visit the Tuolumne County Museum and History Center, 158 W. Bradford Street. This compact museum will introduce you to the Gold Rush era through its collection of period maps, mining equipment, gold ore, and documents of community history, and its changing exhibits.

◆ Tour the Sonora Hebrew Cemetery (Yaney and Oak Streets).

◆ Walk on Linoberg Street, named for Emanuel Linoberg, and cross the street to see the remaining iron letters of Linoberg's name on his former building at 87 S. Washington. Proceed to the former Baer Store, 105 S. Washington, founded in 1851 by Meyer Baer.

◆ Walk Washington Street to get the flavor of a Gold Country town.

*Tour option:*
◆ Visit Jamestown, one mile south-

west of Sonora, and its historic Rail Town.

*Travel to Columbia State Historic Park.*

### Columbia State Historical Park

◆ The Park is an enticing lunch stop. Picnic tables and restaurants are available.

◆ Spend one or two hours in this accurately restored Gold Rush town enjoying such sights as the museum, Wells Fargo Express, Fallon House Theater, pharmacy, the Chinese Joss House, firehouse, and City Hotel. You may want to pan for gold or take a stagecoach ride.

◆ Visit the scenes of Jewish community life in the 1850s and 1860s. On Main Street, walk by the New York Dry Goods Store, once owned by Phillip Schwartz, and the adjacent stores of the Levy families. Nearby, the Masonic temple once housed the Jewish High Holiday services. Group tours can be arranged in advance through the Park Ranger.

*Travel to Mokelumne Hill.*

*Tour options (Columbia to Mokelumne Hill):*

◆ Walk along Main Street of Angels Camp (Main Street is also Highway 49 which goes through Angels Camp).

◆ Explore the charming Gold Rush town of Murphys.

◆ Tour the limestone Mercer Caverns in Murphys.

◆ Visit the Calaveras County Museum at 30 N. Main Street, San Andreas.

## Mokelumne Hill

◆ Tour the Mokelumne Hill Jewish Cemetery (Center Street in the Protestant Cemetery).

*Travel to Jackson.*

## Jackson

◆ Tour Givoth Olam (Hills of Eternity) (Cemetery Road off Placer).

◆ Visit the former site of the B'nai Israel Synagogue, founded in 1857. The site is marked by a plaque at Church and North Streets.

◆ Visit the Amador County Museum at 225 Church Street, housed in an 1859 home. Look for the landscape painting of Jackson in 1880 by Ivy Yarrington which shows the B'nai Israel Synagogue. Take the tour of a model of the Kennedy Mine (part of the museum).

*Tour option:*
◆ Visit the Kennedy Mine Tailings Wheels, Jackson Gate Road.

*End of first day.* Lodging and meals are available in surrounding communities, including Jackson, Amador City, Sutter Creek or in Placerville, the start of the tour for Day Two.

DAY TWO:
JACKSON TO NEVADA CITY

*Travel to Placerville.*

## Placerville

◆ Tour the Placerville Jewish Cemetery (Myrtle and Myrtle Lane).

◆ Walk Main Street noticing the Round Tent Store at 384 Main, once a Gold Rush dry goods store with a number of Jewish owners, among them Caroline Tannenwald of Cincinnati, who bought the store in 1853, and possibly Henry Greenberg, the first President of the Placerville Hebrew Benevolent Society.

*Tour option:*
◆ Visit site of original Placerville synagogue, Congregation B'nai B'rith, on the corner of Cottage and El Dorado Streets. This synagogue burned in 1878 after which a second site was purchased on Mill Street, though the congregation was later dissolved and the property sold.

*Travel to Nevada City.*

*Tour option:*
◆ Visit Marshall Gold Discovery State Historical Park, Coloma. This can be a picnic spot for lunch.

## Nevada City

◆ Walk the downtown, noting the architecture and historic sights including the Nevada Theater, National Hotel, Firehouse I (now the Nevada County Museum),

Firehouse II, and the hydraulic monitor.

• Pass by the Baruh home at 516 Main Street, built in 1852 by Nevada City Jewish merchant Aaron Baruh. The home is not open to the public.

• Tour the Nevada City Jewish Cemetery (Searls Avenue near Walrath Street).

*Tour option:*

• Tour the Malakoff Diggings State Historical Park, with its hydraulic mining site, exhibits, and museum.

*End of Second Day.* Lodging and meals are available in surrounding communities including Nevada City and adjacent Grass Valley.

DAY THREE:
NEVADA CITY TO SACRAMENTO

*Travel to Grass Valley.*

## Grass Valley

• Tour Shaar Zedek Cemetery (Second and Eureka Streets).

• Walk Main Street and adjacent historic area, noting the Holbrooke Hotel, once host to Mark Twain and General Ulysses S. Grant.

• Tour the Empire Mine State Historical Park.

*Tour option:*

• It is possible to combine a lunch stop and a tour of the Northstar Mining Museum.

*Travel to Marysville.*

## Marysville

• Tour the Marysville Hebrew Cemetery (Highway 70, just north of town).

• View the possible site of Congregation B'nai B'rith on the east side of C Street between First and Second Street.

• Visit the site of the Chinese Bok Kai Temple, D Street at the Yuba River levee.

*Travel to Sacramento.*

## Sacramento

• Tour Old Town, including the California State Railroad Museum and the Discovery Museum.

• Tour Home of Peace, B'nai Israel Jewish Cemetery (on Stockton Street) with emphasis on the Gold Rush Era gravestones. Be sure to call Temple Israel for entry arrangements.

*Tour option:*

• Tour the California State Capitol.

*End of Day Three. End of your tour of pioneer Jewish cemeteries of the Gold Rush.*

## *The New Generation of Gold Rush Country Jewish Communities*

Congregation B'nai Harim
P.O. Box 2544
Placerville, CA 95667
(916) 644-5122

Foothill Jewish Community of
Amador County
P.O. Box 1625
Jackson, CA 95642
(209) 223-5750

Mother Lode Jewish Community
P.O. Box 4411
Sonora, California 95370

Nevada County Jewish
Community Center
506 Walsh Street
Grass Valley, California 95945
(916) 268-8101

Gravestone of Samuel Snow. Placerville Jewish
Cemetery. Photo: Ira Nowinksi/Judah L.
Magnes Museum. Western Jewish History
Center.

# ❧ BIBLIOGRAPHY ❧

## Primary Sources

Western Jewish History Center,
Judah L. Magnes Museum,
Berkeley, CA.

Glazier Family Collection
Robert Levinson Collection
Marcuse Collection
Zellerbach Collection

American Jewish Archives,
Cincinnati, Ohio

American Jewish Historical Society
Archives, Waltham, Massachusetts

## Secondary Sources

Bean, Walton and James Rawls.
*California An Interpretive History*
5th ed. New York: McGraw-Hill,
1988.

Benjamin, I.J. *Three Years in America:
1859–1862.* Volumes I and II.
Translated by Charles Reznikoff.
Philadelphia: Jewish Publication
Society of America, 1956.

Brown, Thomas P. *Colorful California
Names* . San Francisco: American
Trust Company, 1957.

Cenotto, Larry. *Logan's Alley,*
Volumes I and II. Jackson,CA.:
Cenotto Publications, 1981.

*Encyclopedia Judaica,* Volumes 2–16.
Jerusalem, Israel: The Macmillan
Company, by Keter Publishing
House Ltd., 1972.

Feingold, Henry (ed.), *The Jewish
People in America,* 5 volumes.
Baltimore: The Johns Hopkins
University Press, for the American
Jewish Historical society, 1992.

Glanz, Rudolf *The Jews of California,
from the Discovery of Gold until
1880.* New York: Waldon Press,
Inc., 1960.

Janicot, Michel, "The Jewish Cemetery
of Grass Valley, California,"
*Western States Jewish Historical
Quarterly,* July, 1988, Vol. XX,
No. 4, 325–333.

Janicot, Michel, "The Jewish Cemetery
of Nevada City, California,"
*Western States Jewish Historical
Quarterly,* October, 1988, Vol.
XXI, No. 1, 58–66.

Levinson, Robert E. *Pioneer Jewish
Cemeteries and Communities of
the California Mother Lode.*
Oakland, CA.: Commission for the
Preservation of Pioneer Jewish
Cemeteries and Landmarks, Magnes
Memorial Museum, 1964.

Levinson, Robert E. *The Jews in the
California Gold Rush.* Berkeley,
CA: Commission for the
Preservation of Pioneer Jewish
Cemeteries and Landmarks of the
Judah L. Magnes Museum,
Berkeley, 1994.

Martin, Don and Betty. *The Best of the
Gold Country.* Columbia, CA.: Pine
Cone Press, 1992.

Pacquette, Mary Grace. "The Other
Harris Levy" CHISPA, *The
Quarterly of The Tuolumne County
Historical Society,* Vol. 32, No. !.
Sonora, 1992.

Paden, Irene and Schlightmann, Margaret. *The Big Oak Flat Road to Yosemite, an account of freighting from Stockton to Yosemite Valley.* Yosemite National Park: Yosemite Natural History Association, 1959.

Rafael, Ruth Kelson. *Western Jewish History Center Guide to Archival and Oral History Collections.* Berkeley: Western Jewish History Center, Judah L. Magnes Memorial Museum, 1987.

Rischin, Moses and John Livingston, eds. *Jews of the American West.* Detroit: Wayne State University Press, 1991.

Rochlin, Harriet and Fred. *Pioneer Jews, A New Life in the Far West.* Boston: Houghton Mifflin Co., 1984.

Sharfman, I. Harold. *Nothing Left to Commemorate.* Glendale, CA.: Arthur H. Clark and Co., 1969.

## *Additional Resources for Tour of Pioneer Jewish Cemeteries*

Video: Chayes, Bill, director and Kahn, Ava, original research. *Birth of a Community, Jews and the Gold Rush.* Berkeley, CA.: Western Jewish History Center of the Judah L. Magnes Museum, 1994.

Brenner, Leslie, ed. Kahn, Ava. *Birth of a Community, Jews and the Gold Rush, A Teacher's Resource Guide for Grades 4–6, 7–9, 10–Adult.* Berkeley: Western Jewish History Center of the Judah L. Magnes Museum, 1995.

Gravestone of Grace [?] Nevada City Jewish Cemetery. Photo: Ira Nowinksi/Judah L. Magnes Museum. Western Jewish History Center.

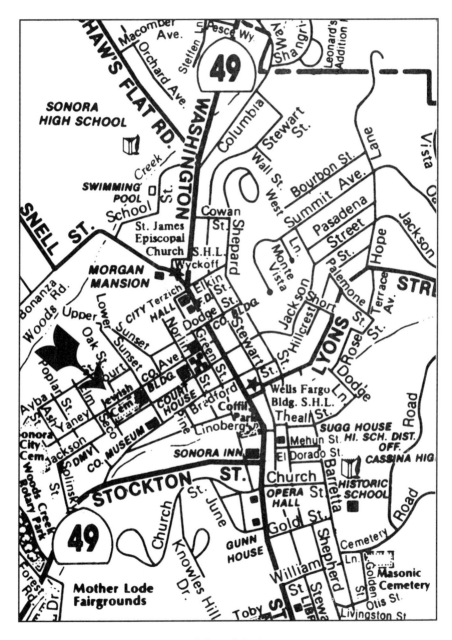

**SONORA**

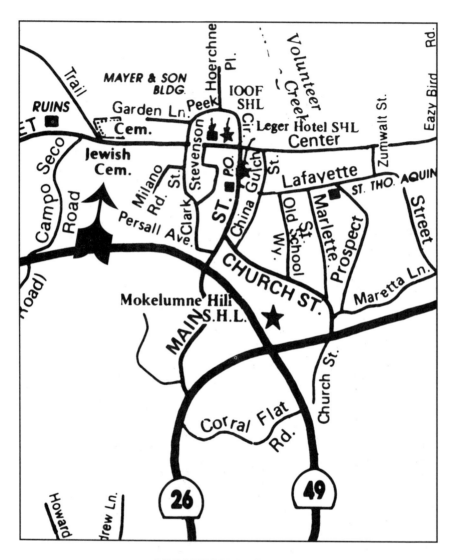

**MOKELUMNE HILL**

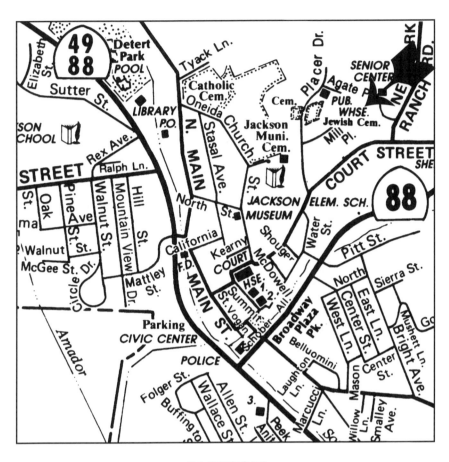

**JACKSON**

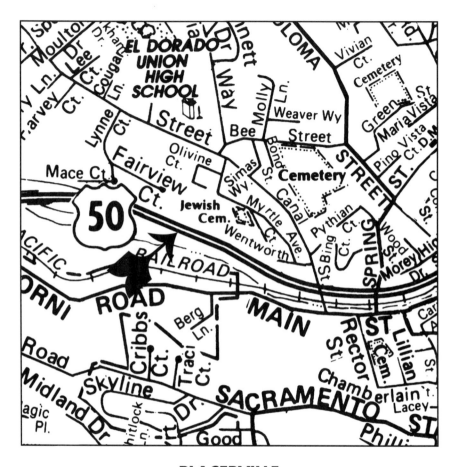

**PLACERVILLE**

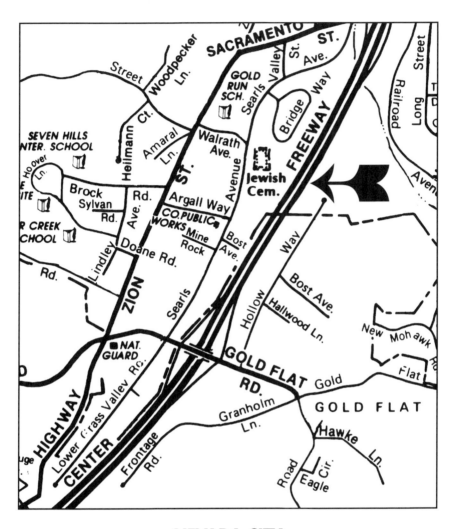

**NEVADA CITY**

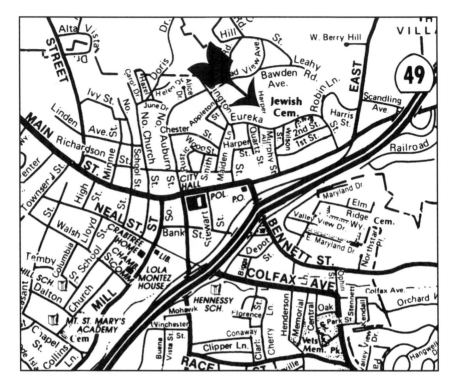

# GRASS VALLEY

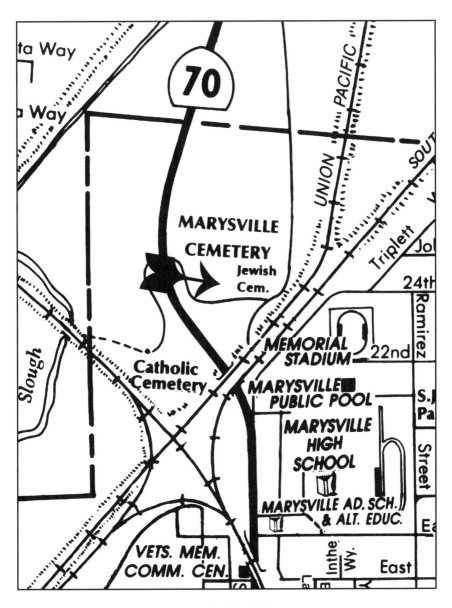

**MARYSVILLE**

# ❧ ABOUT THE AUTHOR ❧

SUSAN MORRIS, an archivist and oral historian with the Western Jewish History Center of the Judah L. Magnes Museum, has an M.A. in history from San Francisco State University and a B.A. in sociology from University of California at Los Angeles. Her long standing interest in western Jewish history perhaps stems from the pioneer heritage passed down from all sides of her family. Her maternal great-great-grandfather, Henry Greenberg, was the first president of the Placerville Hebrew Benevolent Society and associated with Placerville's Round Tent Store. Her grandfather, Harry Hilp Sr., grandson of Henry Greenberg, was the first treasurer of the Commission for the Preservation of the Pioneer Jewish Cemeteries and Landmarks. The Herman Furst, brother-in-law of Isadore Sokolowski who is buried in the Mokelumne Hill Jewish Cemetery, is Susan's paternal great-grandfather. Her husband, Mark, is also a descendent of California pioneer Jewish families. His great-grandfather, Abe Haines' first wife, Rachel Haines, is buried in the Jackson cemetery and in the 1870s, another great-grandfather, Aaron Harris, ran the first pack station in the Yosemite Valley. Susan and Mark Morris live in Marin County and have two grown children.

Placerville, circa 1860. Aaron and Mathilda Hilp Kahn. Courtesy of Betsy Klein Schwartz.

# Kaddish

*Kaddish* is Aramaic for holy. The Mourner's *Kaddish*, recited by the closest relatives of the deceased at the burial and each day during the seven days of mourning, carries with it the hope that the piety of the mourners may have a redeeming influence on behalf of the deceased. The prayer is also traditionally recited with congregational responses at the close of daily prayers in the synagogue.

*Kaddish* is not a prayer for the dead, nor a supplication, nor an expression of one's personal grief, rather it is a prayer which praises God and looks beyond the personal to a new and better life for all mankind.

יִתְגַּדַּל וְיִתְקַדַּשׁ שְׁמֵהּ רַבָּא בְּעָלְמָא דִּי־בְרָא כִרְעוּתֵהּ,
וְיַמְלִיךְ מַלְכוּתֵהּ בְּחַיֵּיכוֹן וּבְיוֹמֵיכוֹן וּבְחַיֵּי דְכָל־בֵּית
יִשְׂרָאֵל, בַּעֲגָלָא וּבִזְמַן קָרִיב, וְאִמְרוּ: אָמֵן.
יְהֵא שְׁמֵהּ רַבָּא מְבָרַךְ לְעָלַם וּלְעָלְמֵי עָלְמַיָּא.
יִתְבָּרַךְ וְיִשְׁתַּבַּח, וְיִתְפָּאַר וְיִתְרוֹמַם וְיִתְנַשֵּׂא, וְיִתְהַדָּר
וְיִתְעַלֶּה וְיִתְהַלָּל שְׁמֵהּ דְּקוּדְשָׁא, בְּרִיךְ הוּא, לְעֵלָּא מִן־כָּל־
בִּרְכָתָא וְשִׁירָתָא, תֻּשְׁבְּחָתָא וְנֶחֱמָתָא דַּאֲמִירָן בְּעָלְמָא,
וְאִמְרוּ: אָמֵן.
יְהֵא שְׁלָמָא רַבָּא מִן־שְׁמַיָּא וְחַיִּים עָלֵינוּ וְעַל־כָּל־יִשְׂרָאֵל,
וְאִמְרוּ: אָמֵן.
עֹשֶׂה שָׁלוֹם בִּמְרוֹמָיו, הוּא יַעֲשֶׂה שָׁלוֹם עָלֵינוּ וְעַל־כָּל־
יִשְׂרָאֵל, וְאִמְרוּ: אָמֵן.

*Let the glory of God be extolled, let His great name be hallowed, in the world whose creation He willed. May His kingdom soon prevail, in our own day, our own lives, and the life of all Israel, and let us say: Amen.*

*Let His great name be blessed for ever and ever.*

*Let the name of the Holy One, blessed is He, be glorified, exalted, and honored, though He is beyond all the praises, songs, and adorations that we can utter, and let us say: Amen.*

*For us and for all Israel, may the blessing of peace and the promise of life come true, and let us say: Amen*

*May He who causes peace to reign in the high heavens, let peace descend on us, on all Israel, and all the world, and let us say: Amen.*